COPING
with the
MALE EGO
in the
WORKPLACE

*Sandra Grymes
and Mary Stanton*

LONGMEADOW
P R E S S

For our grandmothers,
mothers,
sisters,
aunts,
and special daughters

Copyright © 1993 by SANDRA GRYMES AND MARY STANTON
Published by Longmeadow Press, 201 High Ridge Road, Stamford, CT 06904.
All rights reserved. No part of this book may be reproduced
or utilized in any form or by any means,
electronic or mechanical, including photocopying, recording or by
any information storage and retrieval system,
without permission in writing from the Publisher.

Longmeadow Press and the colophon are registered trademarks.

Although portions of this book are derived from real events,
each character in it is fictional,
a composite drawn from several individuals and from
the authors' imaginations.
No reference to any real person is intended or should be inferred.

Library of Congress Cataloging-in-Publication Data
Grymes, Sandra.
    Coping with the male ego in the workplace /
  by Sandra Grymes and Mary Stanton.
      p.   cm.   Includes bibliographical references and index.
    1. Sex role in the work environment–United States.
    2. Sex discrimination against women–United States.
    3. Women–United States–Psychology.
    4. Men–United States–Psychology.
    5. Women–Employment–United States.
  I. Stanton, Mary. II. Title.
  HD6060.5.U5G79 1993 305.33–dc20   93-15362
  ISBN 0-681-41454-5

Cover design by Kelvin P. Oden
Interior design by Donna R. Miller
Printed in United States
First Edition
0 9 8 7 6 5 4 3 2 1

Contents

Women hold up half the sky.
Chinese Proverb

Life for me ain't been no crystal stair.
Langston Hughes

Acknowledgments

When we asked women and men to talk with us about coping with the male ego in the workplace, each laughed knowingly. There was no lack of eagerness to be interviewed! Each told her or his experience and each tale had a familiar ring. A special thank you to all of our reporters who shared with us their frustrations, insights, and prescriptions.

To our editor, Adrienne Ingrum, we owe a special debt of gratitude for her guidance as the work progressed and especially for the excited phone call one Sunday morning to exclaim that she loved the book.

We applaud Donna Kitt who transformed our diskettes into draft after draft and helped us to meet each deadline.

We extend our deepest appreciation to our families and friends who offered their support and encouragement.

Finally, we thank the two women who served us well as interpreters of their time—our mothers. They and the extended family of their generation taught us, each in her own way, that the world could be ours and that the hurdle of gender should never dampen our dreams.

1

Windows on the Workplace

"In soloing—as in other activities—it is far easier to start something than it is to finish it."

Amelia Earhart

JEANETTE

Jeanette is a forty-year-old vice president of development for a private sector agency. She administers a $3.5 million budget and a staff of eighteen. "I was desperate to fill a direct mail campaign director's position that had been vacant for six months. It had turned over twice in as many years. My candidate had been a fund-raising vice president earlier in his career, and seemed willing to take the relatively low salary that I could offer only because he wanted to get back into the workforce. I knew something was wrong five minutes into the interview," she says. "I felt that same deep-in-the-belly uneasiness that I'd experienced the day I married my first husband. I ignored it then, too. I told myself I was just being silly. Over the banging of my internal alarm I offered him a job.

"The next six months were heaven. Dave organized the failing department and increased not only the productivity, but the visibility of the one area in my division where I had the least personal expertise. I confided that to him during a glowing performance review. A big mistake.

"When his staff went over his head to complain to me that he had a volatile temper, disciplined them publicly, and made their working lives hell, I discounted it. I chose instead to accept his version—that they didn't like being supervised, they were undisciplined. I even felt uncomfortable bringing the subject up with him. After all, contributions were up and staff complaints were down under his direction.

"Gradually he began to take more and more independent action. He missed staff meetings, cancelled appointments, and called to say that he was spending the day 'in the field.' When I confronted him he reminded me, with a smile, that he had a job comparable with mine at another agency not so long ago. He knew fund-raising inside out, he assured me. 'Did I think that he was keeping things from me?' he asked, apparently horrified. 'No, no, I mumbled, just try to keep me a little more informed. . . . He apologized again and said he would.

"Next, he began to take his subordinates and colleagues to lunch and charge it to the agency. This was something I had never permitted my other directors—both women—to do. Still, I hesitated to bring it to his attention. When I finally did, he assured me it was an accepted business practice in other organizations, yet, if I objected he certainly understood and would stop immediately. I won the point, but felt somehow diminished.

"Then he registered for a professional conference in Atlanta. When I questioned him about it, he assured me that it was crucial he attend. He had to keep current. Again, he reminded me it was important that 'the organization' build competence in direct mail fund-raising. I had refused both female directors conferences that year, but I backed down and signed off on his. The subtle references to my deficiencies hit home. It somehow didn't matter to me that I was the boss—that I successfully managed a division. I had done reasonably well keeping the area going during the six-month vacancy before Dave arrived. I began to focus on the disaster that could have happened (but didn't) and felt dependent on Dave's decision making.

"I deferred to his judgment in hiring outside consultants to assist us in creating a new direct mail campaign. Although I knew the agency frowned on the use of consultants because money was so tight, I signed what was essentially an open-ended agreement. By year's end we came in almost a quarter of a million dollars over budget.

"When I look back I get so angry," Jeanette says, her eyes dark and flashing. "I let him deal with my boss directly, I allowed him, in fact I *helped* him build a reputation for being more competent than I was. I had the power and the ability to stop this at any point, and yet I let it happen. I let him assume authority, treat people unfairly, and promote himself in a way that I would never have allowed the female directors to do.

"To make a long story short, all our projects got accomplished, the fund-raising department got stabilized, and I got fired for not watching the bottom line. My other directors shed no tears. They had gotten very little support from me during that year, and they took a lot of abuse from him. He made no secret of his disdain for them, and assured me that their incompetence was dragging our division down and making both of us look bad. Can you believe it? The tragedy was that I allowed my self-esteem to dip so low that I began to believe it too. The more he subtly questioned my ability, the more I invested in him. I gave up my power and sought his approval! I became more and more dependent on him and more distrustful of the rest of my staff.

"If I hadn't let things get so distorted I'd still have my job," Jeanette says regretfully. "If I had just used the power that was mine to supervise him effectively, I'd still have my job. I'm still in shock. This didn't happen because his ego was so strong," she says. "It happened because mine was so weak–I let him walk all over me."

KAY

Having to fire a favored male is not an enviable position for a female executive. It is especially delicate when the male is one of the "boys," and has an amicable relationship with the CEO. Kay, the senior vice president of a manufacturing company, faced a dilemma fraught with political overtones.

Sam was different from Kay's other direct reports in that he was hired for his technical skills and industry contacts over his managerial skills, which the company thought he could develop. He was charged with starting a new product in a very competitive environment. If the product succeeded, the CEO expected to rise in the corporation.

The CEO was a man who liked risks and saw himself as a maverick vis-à-vis the parent company. He was obsessive about control and meddled in the affairs of his direct reports.

Sam took up more and more with a group of managers who were part of the "old boy's" network. This group not only knew the company's history, but was adept at getting around its rules. He came to know the war stories and to see the heroes as the boys who "got over." The old boys were viewed by the brightest and the best as foolish and unprepared. Sam never embraced this attitude. Instead, he felt committed to proving that he could balance his relationship with this group very nicely with the expectations of his workgroup.

For many months, Kay had been feeling uneasy about Sam's performance. There was something cavalier about his version of events, and Kay found herself asking for more detail and documentation of his analysis of his business. His response to her requests was to complain about time pressures.

Sam enjoyed a privileged relationship with the CEO, who met him in the hall every morning, often commented on the work, gave him direction, and let him know that he should get business wherever he could, even if it meant the rules were stretched. Over time, Sam played to the CEO.

Sam would always tell Kay the content of his discussions with the CEO. In so doing, it was evident that he also had gained the feeling that the CEO was the only person he had to please and that it was okay to break innocuous rules.

The CEO and Kay had several confrontations around his giving direction to Sam since what he would request would sometimes be out of line with the larger goal or the bigger picture for the unit. He knew she didn't like his giving directions to the staff she supervised. He explained he could not help himself, saw it as his prerogative, and continued to do it with her group as well as with others.

Sam met his revenue goals the first year of the business. He was a hero in the eyes of the CEO. Although the revenue goals were met, Kay felt Sam had run his operation like a one-man show by neglecting its administrative underpinnings and ignoring his staff's development.

He also had an argument with the parent company about a manufacturing policy that it planned to implement and with which he disagreed. When he discussed it with Kay, she told him to produce whatever evidence he had to substantiate his point of view, but when the policy was finalized he had to follow it whether or not he agreed.

Sam thought the company's decision makers were being silly. When their decision countered his own judgment, he circumvented company policy and manufactured the product in accordance with the specifications he thought were better. He did not think he would be caught so he did not try to bury the evidence of his wrongdoing. He believed that his actions would not jeopardize the public safety and would help his bottom line.

The first sign of trouble began when a new corporate officer was hired. His need to distinguish himself before the other corporate officers motivated him to quickly identify a compelling situation. Word of Sam's manufacturing decision was leaked to him. He put the pressure on Sam's CEO to explain to the parent company the local deviations from the manufacturing policy.

The CEO talked with Sam who owned up to what he had done and was convinced that he had behaved expeditiously. When the CEO reached Kay, who was away on company business, he frantically insisted that she return immediately to deal with the situation.

Kay was alarmed because it was obvious there were too many vested interests being played out here. She knew the CEO was expecting a major promotion and would not appreciate any attention that would thwart his chances. Additionally, Kay did not want any of her units to be perceived as being out of control.

When Kay arrived, she met with Sam to find out his version of events. He acknowledged that he had made a decision which he felt was right. He knew it was against both company policy and her instruction. He knew he would be reprimanded for this and expected a slap on the wrist and business as usual.

When Kay met with the CEO, he explained what he had been told and presented the documentation gathered by the parent company. He was uncomfortable with these developments because he knew they were rife with organizational politics. Kay told him what she knew about the situation and when she knew it. He expressed his disappointment with Sam especially since he was relied upon for his technical skill.

He asked her how they should handle Sam. Kay said they should terminate him.

The CEO looked as if he were in pain, but he did not argue with Kay. When she sensed his hesitation, she said Sam should be fired because he had broken a company policy and he had put the CEO in a vulnerable position vis-à-vis the corporation. The CEO weakly assured Kay that he could handle his position. Kay acknowledged she was sure that he could, but Sam should be fired nonetheless. He asked her to meet with the vice president of human resources to work out a week's suspension, during which the parent company planned to conduct a full-scale audit of Sam's operation.

The vice president, Kay, and the corporation's lawyer worked out the best way to handle Sam's suspension. When Kay told Sam they were suspending him for one week without pay, he was furious. He understood their need to punish him. Sending him home for one week was bad enough, not paying him was more than he could take. He wanted to see the CEO to discuss it with him.

Kay and the vice president reported the conversation with Sam to the CEO who asked how he should treat this situation. The vice president told him that it would be helpful if he supported the decision to suspend Sam without pay.

The CEO met with Sam who pleaded his case effectively. The CEO told him that if the lawyers agreed to a suspension with pay then he would support it. The lawyers, however, defined a suspension with pay as a vacation. When the week expired, the company decided that Sam needed to be off-site for another day because the audit report was not finished.

Kay called Sam to inform him of this decision. Sam said he had checked with his lawyer who said the company had no right to do this to him. He said he would resign or be terminated. He wanted a sizable severance package and insisted on returning to work, emphasizing that they could not stop him.

When Sam returned to work, the "old boys" were glad to see him and invited him for coffee. He told them what was happening to him and they downplayed his predicament. They offered examples of others who had overcome the CEO's displeasure. They also reassured him that he would get a healthy severance package if he were asked to resign.

In the meeting with Kay and the vice president, Sam tried to set a light tone by making a joke about how quickly the week had gone by. The vice president asked him why he had come to work when he was asked to remain home. He repeated what he had told Kay. After some discussion, Kay terminated him without severance pay.

GAIL

Two years ago Gail was director of ambulatory care for a large metropolitan hospital. Gail's boss, Ken Whitten, who was administrator for professional services, had given her the responsibility for implementing a new clinic procedure that he had designed. His goal was to schedule patients and move them through the clinics within a maximum waiting time of two hours. Gail told Ken at the outset that this wasn't possible. The current wait was over four hours, the systems were archaic, and a two-hour cutback was unrealistic. He was furious. He had just started his job and wanted to be a hero.

"If you can't take charge of those clinics and get the residents to move those patients through efficiently, I'll find someone who can," he bellowed. Gail told him she'd do her best.

Two weeks later, Gail and two of her clinic supervisors met in Ken's office to review their progress. In the interim, there had been an equipment breakdown in Radiology and patients couldn't be seen for an entire day. The backup had a disastrous effect on scheduling. The waiting time for that two-week period actually increased. Ken was livid.

"You fucking people," he roared. "Can't you do anything right? Who was responsible for rescheduling? Whatever happened to the backup equipment? Why didn't someone tell me before now?" Before anyone could respond, Ken picked up the telephone from his desk and threw it against the wall. Now he had everyone's attention. Gail and the two supervisors sat open-mouthed until they were dismissed. "I don't remember a thing he said after he threw the phone," she says.

"When we walked out I felt like a child. I felt abused and yes, I felt ashamed because I hadn't defended my staff. His violent behavior put us all in shock and I froze.

"The next morning I decided to go to Ken's boss. I saw no point in giving Ken another opportunity to be abusive. One of the supervisors had called in sick, and I suspected that she was looking for a job. The other was so distraught that she was virtually useless that morning.

"I'd been in the workforce for seven years at that point," says Gail, "and I knew how serious it was to go over your boss's head. I just didn't care. If I went to personnel they'd tell me to file a grievance. It would be a long, drawn out procedure and I knew Ken would find a way to trivialize the incident and justify himself before it was over. I wanted to act while the outrage was still fresh.

"Ken's boss, Don Mohr, was the chief operating officer, one level below the top. He agreed to see me right away. He seemed to be listening intently, and I thought sympathetically, until I told him about the telephone. At that point he smiled, 'You think this is funny?' I asked. He flushed. 'No, no,' he assured me. He was embarrassed. His smile had been involuntary and therefore an honest reaction.

"'We're all under pressure,' he offered. 'Whitten's a good man. He shouldn't have done that, but he knows what he's charged with.'

"'Mr. Mohr,' I said, and now I was completely calm, 'that man makes almost $100,000 a year. He should learn to control himself.'

"'That's not the point,' Mohr said tensely.

"'I think it is,' I continued. 'A $20,000 employee would have been fired for doing the same thing. My staff is afraid of him and that's wrong.'

"I knew it was over. While Mohr repeated he was not condoning Whitten's behavior, he wove in the message that the clinic operation had to improve. He *could* not or *would* not separate the issues. Whitten had just gotten a little 'overzealous.'

"Mohr essentially told me to get cracking. He advised me to get the supervisors pulling together to accomplish the goal so that the level of frustration would decrease and there wouldn't be so much tension in the air. He actually wanted me to fix it! Given an unrealistic goal under the guidance of an abusive supervisor, Mohr's advice to me was to try to understand Whitten's position! Mohr was neither sarcastic nor nasty. He believed he was giving me good advice.

"Both supervisors resigned six months before I left to work as a clinic management consultant. Whitten went through two clinic directors after me. Four months ago, he left to accept a job as CEO of a suburban hospital: Last I heard the patients were still waiting an average of five hours for medical attention."

CINDY

Cindy, a copywriter for an advertising agency, says she sometimes feels invisible and at other times wishes she could be.

"We were going to a lunch meeting with a new client," Cindy begins. "It was important to impress this client because we had lost three big accounts in the last six months and as a result had suffered a 20 percent agency cutback. Thirty-eight people across the board were laid off. I felt lucky to be assigned any account. I felt lucky to have kept my job.

"There were four of us. Two account executives from my agency and a brand manager, all meeting with a marketing executive from the account. I was the only representative from my agency's 'creative side.' I also was the only female.

"As soon as we were seated the football talk began. Last Sunday's game was replayed in maddening detail. There was endless speculation about who was 'finished,' who needed to be traded, and who wasn't pulling his weight. It continued until they felt comfortable with each other. Unfortunately, I had little to offer. The best I could do was ask a few questions, and that didn't help. I felt awkward and impotent. I could see by the time we got around to the presentation my position as 'outsider' would be set. They were bonding the hell out of each other.

"As coffee was being served, the brand manager told our senior account executive that he had the 'material' Ben had requested. He had an irritating smile on his face as he passed a piece of paper across the table to Ben. Ben thanked him, smiling broadly as he began to read aloud a series of 'dumb blonde' jokes. He read eight of them. I felt my body go rigid. I glared at Ben, but he would not make eye contact. My pride began to wrestle violently with my overdrawn checking account. Stop him? Get up and walk out? Try to humiliate him? It was too late. He was finished and they were all guffawing. I was as invisible as I had been during the football preliminaries.

"During lunch I had been away from the table for almost ten minutes calling in copy changes. There had been ample time to do this while I was gone.

"I was so angry–at Ben and at myself. I was ashamed for not having taken a stand and at the same time confused. What was the right thing to do when I needed this job so desperately? I had a ten-year-old son besides myself to think about. It was exhausting. Ben knew. I knew that he knew. I could talk with him privately, but he had the power to take me off the account. "When I got back to the agency my mind was racing. I couldn't stand myself. Jim, my art director partner, was still at his desk. We had become good friends. I considered Jim an enlightened male. He had a reputation in the agency as a strong advocate for women's issues. I laid it all out for him, keeping just this side of hysteria. He looked confused–honestly confused–and a little scared.

"'Cindy,'" he said, 'don't blow this for us. If our team is taken off the account, then we're expendable. Maybe you're being a little too sensitive about this one.'"

MOIRA

Moira was the special assistant to the president of a national chain of sporting goods stores.

She had excellent organizational and analytical skills, met her deadlines, and produced exemplary work. She handled a wide variety of assignments including some of the president's personal business and often had to interpret the president's wishes to the franchise manager, vice presidents, and other staff. Her interpersonal skills were adequate to the tasks of keeping the company's owners informed and at some distance from the day-to-day management decision making. Some assignments required that she travel to meetings with the president.

Moira worked diligently and matched the president in commitment to the company and to the tasks at hand. They both arrived at work at 7:30 A.M.; they worked twelve-hour days.

Moira was intent on developing her skills so she could advance in the company to a top-level position. She wanted to run a company franchise.

The president became increasingly dependent on Moira, often seeking her advice and counsel. Each evening they would discuss the day's work and relive its challenges. Moira became his confidante. Besides the work, they talked about the problems she was having with her ex-husband and son, and he shared with her the problems in his marriage.

Within six months, Moira and the president were engrossed in an affair.

Over the next two years, Moira became the most powerful woman in the company and the gatekeeper to the president. She was able to discern the power of others and interpret for him whom he needed to cultivate. She would act as a partner to him in this regard. He relied on her to give him advice and counsel regarding the politics of the job. Gradually, she functioned like his alter ego. She tried to keep her personal relationship separate from the tasks of the job; however, she admitted this was difficult, as she came to know the president and he became so dependent on her.

The vice presidents resented her for being able to wield her power. One competed with her for the boss's favor. Another was smitten by her charm and envied the boss's conquest.

The women walked around her gingerly. Some tended to discount her abilities, but that was difficult because she was a very competent person who did her homework and always delivered for the president.

The president was pleased with her productivity and clearly was delighted with Moira. He arranged his schedule to spend as much time with her as possible, supported her ideas in meetings, reprimanded people who were critical of her, gave her increasing responsibility, and brought her flowers and other tokens of his affection. He made few decisions before discussing them thoroughly with her.

In spite of Moira being very circumspect about her personal relationship with the president, word of a romantic liaison spread throughout the organization.

Staff members began to report that Moira and the president were seen leaving the office together after hours and often lunched at a favorite neighborhood pub. At a trade meeting he was observed at dinner nuzzling her hair.

She tried to get him to be more discreet. She thought he was a little careless, especially when he could not control his desire for her and kissed her in the company parking lot.

For him it was a badge of honor to have attracted this beautiful, talented, understanding woman who could be relied on to execute his wishes and demands. She was his trophy and he knew he was envied by other men on the staff as well as the owners.

Moira's assignments were broad ranging enough that she gained an appreciation for how the business was run. She was privy to company secrets and the president's agenda. She made it clear to the vice presidents and the franchise manager that talking to her was the same as talking to the president.

The president instructed his vice presidents to pass their work by Moira for review. Moira assumed more power; she gave direction.

Since she was responsible for coordinating the operational plan, she recognized the deficiencies in the franchise area.

When the vice presidents were slack about getting their work in on time or completing a task, Moira stepped in to see it was done. Sometimes she did it herself. Soon, she was doing pieces of other staff member's jobs. Although she could assess the technical side of an operation correctly, her conclusions misfired often because she missed the politics.

The president allowed her to assume more power and ignored the growing tension and hostility of his vice presidents. None of the vice presidents directly confronted the president about their anger toward him or Moira. They grumbled and complained among themselves.

Although there was general agreement that the franchise manager was not on top of his areas, Moira decided that she would see to it that he was replaced. Over a three-month period, Moira pointed out repeatedly the shortcomings of the franchise manager who began to have nasty exchanges with Moira in the staff meetings. The president used Moira's dissatisfaction with the franchise manager as a means to express his own disregard for his work. Moira began to put pressure on the president to fire him. He became irritated and was upset with her for insisting on the franchise manager's removal.

Moira couldn't understand why he was so upset since his shortcomings were obvious to everyone and he had complained to her that the franchise manager often was overwhelmed.

Their disagreement over the issue turned into a fight, which began to creep into the staff meetings with the vice presidents. Other disagreements between them became public.

After two years, the tide turned in their relationship when she began to criticize him publicly and tell him how to run his business. After the franchise manager resigned voluntarily, several of the owners, who knew the president well, began to question him about his relationship with Moira.

The president denied that he was having an affair with Moira. Subsequently, he and Moira argued, and he broke off the affair. He continued to expect her to produce the work and give him advice. Moira found the situation untenable. The people she had run over when she had more authority now ignored her. Although she and the president had a tense truce, it was clear she was not going anywhere with the president or the job, so she resigned.

The president went from having a trophy in this woman whom he had empowered, to the point where he argued with her and she screamed at him in public.

Moira was distraught when she left the company. She worried whether her emotional investment in the president and all those hours she had given to the job and to him were worth it. She wondered about sex in the workplace.

Moira maintained that the relationship was only a side part of the job, the foundation was her own competence. In the end, she discovered that her legitimate authority ended when the affair ended.

ROSE

Rose was Daddy's girl. Being the youngest child and the only daughter, her father doted on her. She was taught by both parents that she had to defer to her father, a successful entrepreneur. He was the authority figure.

When she married, Rose's mother gave up her own dreams to be a schoolteacher. Whenever she had worked, it was to earn extra money or to help her husband advance his educational or business goals.

Her mother believed that women were dependent on their husbands and owed them a certain respect. Rose observed her mother as she reaffirmed, took care of, and catered to her father.

Mother was a competent and nurturing woman who managed the family's finances and determined its life style. She pushed her older sons' ambitions more than her daughter's. She expected Rose to marry after college and to have a life similar to her own.

Rose had three older brothers. What they were doing was always intriguing to her, and she trailed them. Like Rose, one of her brothers was good at math and science, and he liked to teach her what he learned. Rose decided she wanted to study engineering like her brother.

Rose's father encouraged her intellectual ability and was proud of her accomplishments, including her success on the swim team. As she matured in her engineering career, he became more of a mentor.

Rose's mother was ambivalent about her daughter's success and worried that she was postponing marriage. When they talked, her mother always asked her about the men in her life, her friend's children, fashion, or how she was wearing her hair.

When Rose went to work, she noted men were treated differently from women: they were catered to, they were held less accountable for their actions, the women constantly built up their egos, and no one out and out lied to them, but no one told them an offensive or irritating truth. Even her boss's secretary, who was not as business literate as the newer computer-literate hires, was the CEO's office wife and mother. She shielded him from criticism, ran his social calendar, handled errands, listened to his complaints, and bolstered his ego.

She remembered that it took years for her to learn to be assertive in the workplace because of the way she was taught to defer to her father. Often this tendency was reinforced by some older men, with whom she worked, who treated the younger women kindly, the way they treated their daughters.

Early in her career, Rose behaved passively when confronted with provocative or antagonistic situations. A few curse words or a forceful personality would intimidate her. She was afraid to assert herself or ask for what she needed. She understood why men would not take her seriously; after all, she was young and inexperienced. She expressed a rare opinion tentatively, even speaking in a soft voice. It was as if she really believed it was more acceptable to be seen and not heard.

However, as she became more experienced and her abilities were tested, her belief in herself soared. Rose knew that she excelled in her work. She could handle the tough tasks. She assumed more responsibility for her own assertiveness: taking courses, speaking authoritatively, always being prepared. She also recognized her own anger at being treated in a subordinate manner.

Being harassed by several men and being overlooked because of her gender also served to embolden her. Once, when she returned from a vacation a colleague told her, "I missed your humor, your brains, and your breasts." Another time, she had an opportunity for an important career move and was told in her last interview with the prospective employer, "Come on little lady, you know this is not the job for you."

Having a few professional women as role models, as well as a close relationship with her father, plus collegial support from her brother helped her to take more risks and to deal more effectively in a man's world.

Once it was clear to her mother that a career was what was going to make her happy, and that her daughter was really quite accomplished, she relaxed and was able to enjoy Rose's success. The tension between them around these issues subsided. To Rose's surprise and pleasure her mother took an introductory engineering course so that she could talk to her more knowledgeably.

Rose's latest assignment is to manage a huge construction project staffed by several men whom she knows are ready to undermine her authority. She feels somewhat nervous about it, yet sees it as a challenge. Rose knows that it might set off an old pattern of deference, but she feels confident that she can handle herself and the tasks at hand.

2

Gender Challenges

"I think the one lesson I have learned is that there is no substitute for paying attention."

Diane Sawyer

*W*hen we asked women and men to share with us their experiences in "coping with the male ego in the workplace" the response was overwhelming. Every interviewee had a tale or more to tell and they couldn't wait to tell it! Listen to some of their voices:

From a man: "I see the female ego as maternal, taking care of me, gentle, tender, merciful even in the workplace. I expect kinder and more understanding treatment from my female superiors than I would expect from my male superiors."

From a woman: "I think of the male ego as strong, tough, decisive, always appearing to be in control even when he is not. The male ego assumes it is always moving upward. The cowboy mentality: silent, forceful, taking action, never backing off, intent on winning. It is curious that the male ego does not permit signs of softness or sentimentality, all of which are identified with being weak."

From a man: "Women bring a different perspective to the marketplace than men. They have a more rounded perspective, can entertain a broader view, can listen to many sides of an issue, can back away strategically from a fight. They are generally viewed as more concerned about the needs of people. Women bring attributes and attitudes that we men regard as weaknesses."

From a woman: "The male ego is a real and universal obstacle to women in the workplace. The social forces that have shaped the female approach to life bumps head on into the silent western male ego. Women are not expected to be direct, aggressive, strong, tough, or unyielding. What is seen as positive on the male side of the equation is seen as negative on the female side. If she is too tough, she will be described as a bitch."

From a man: "When women joined the newsroom, I didn't think they could cover the news stories or face dangerous situations. I questioned their stamina and courage. I believed they could only handle soft news. I was wrong. I made all the wrong assumptions."

There was wide acceptance of the concept of the male ego. Everyone understood what we meant; their understanding was based on a common experience.

Among working women there is a common exasperation about the way the "male ego" is expressed. This shared frustration cuts across age, class, and racial lines. For example, Margaret Willis is a retired African-American woman with a high school education. When she was asked to describe the male ego she responded immediately. "Always right, never to be questioned. Never, ever to be challenged."

Compare her description with that of Charlotte Hays, a thirty-five-year-old white woman who is a senior vice president of an advertising agency. "He cannot be wrong. There is only one way to do everything, which is his way."

Dr. Sarah Harkin, a forty-eight-year-old African-American pharmacist, expresses the male view of the world this way: "I am powerful. *The* power. Anything you get will be over my dead body or after my approval."

Edna O'Brien, a fifty-five-year-old white hospital nursing director, expresses it as, "the need to put you in your place, to manipulate you or keep you in line through humiliation. One proves his manliness by being able to put the woman in her place."

The very experiences which provoke that kind of anger are often similar. Margaret Willis worked on a production line for a manufacturing firm more than thirty years ago. She offered her foreman a suggestion for improving production in her area and she was ignored.

"I found out two weeks later," she says "that my idea was being presented. I said to the foreman, 'that was my idea.'

"He said, 'What do you mean?'

"I said, 'I showed you how to turn that piece so you would not have to rotate it twice in the same direction.'

" 'Well, I don't know nothing about it,' he said. 'It came from the boss up front.' " Ms. Willis sighs. "They take your idea," she says, "and go quietly away and when they return they present your idea as their own."

Charlotte Hays remembers, "An art director stole an ad I wrote when I was a junior art director. I went to the creative supervisor about it and he told me, 'These things happen.' "

The Male Ego

The male ego is that manifestation of behavior that is a result of a strong need to maintain a sense of superiority and control. It can range from indifference or passively ignoring a woman to capricious or arbitrary behavior. It is reflected in acts that protect male advantage. It is heard in language that others experience as intimidating or humiliating. It is seen in the slant of the shoulders–in the shift of an eye. Some men think this behavior goes unrecognized. Others have little insight into the pain it causes.

The male ego has thrived in the American workplace, tra- ditionally a man's world. As social forces coalesce and approach a critical mass however, American business recognizes a need to change its mode of operation. Male ego driven management styles are losing currency. Management by intimidation is not playing well to today's diverse workforce.

Our sales people, technicians, customer service reps, middle managers, and support staff include large numbers of veterans of the civil rights, feminist, and Vietnam War protest movements. They are *very* clear about human rights issues in the workplace. Younger workers are even less inclined to respond to rigid, forceful, punitive attempts to motivate them. Many of these new workers were raised by the children of the '60s. Their egalitarian values and sense of entitlement drive them to respond to pressure with pressure.

Boss-as-bully just does not cut it anymore, yet traditional autocratic, bureaucratic managers have been slow to understand this. It makes them angry and their solution is simply to apply more force. This mentality has increasingly become a stumbling block to forward-looking executives whose visions of their corporations include substantive operational and behavioral changes.

The balance of power is shifting. The nature of work, the product mix, and consumer demand are all changing. To compete for global markets, American business needs to improve its productivity and satisfy a workforce that will be largely female and minority.

And women must work. For the majority of women in the United States a job is critical. Single women support themselves, married women contribute the crucial second check, and single mothers are responsible for the entire family burden.

Women continue to struggle to make a place for themselves. Consider these statistics:

- About half of all women with children under the age of one year work outside the home. Four out of five single mothers with children under the age of three work.
- New mothers are ten times more likely to lose their jobs after

medical leaves for childbirth than employees taking other kinds of medical leave.

* Although women account for 40 percent of all managers in the United States, only 2 percent of women managers earn more than $50,000 a year compared with 14 percent of the men.
* Less than 11 percent of American women are housewives who do not work outside the home, but are supported by their spouses.
* The average marriage lasts just 9.1 years.
* Only 40 percent of all major corporations have women on their boards of directors, and only 3 percent of all directorships are held by women.
* Women earned 72 cents for every dollar earned by men in 1991. This is only a slight improvement over 1955 when women earned 65 cents for every dollar earned by men.

These are harsh economic realities and women are managing them. In addition to the economic struggle, however, they are also required to cope with the inequities of the workplace. How women cope with these workplace inequities, distortions, and discriminatory practices while protecting their ability to make a living is the subject of our book.

This book is designed to help men and women understand each other and to move beyond anger and frustration. We believe that women can direct their unique strengths into actions that can make the energy of the female ego work to their advantage.

Remember those women who some years ago donned Brooks Brothers suits and adapted the male style of intimidation in their quest for success? Where are they now? Imitating male behavior put those women in a double bind. They tried to shatter the stereotypes of women as non aggressive, non competitive, passive and accommodating. It didn't work. It neither endeared them to the men they were trying to impress, nor to the staff they were trying to manage. They were criticized for the "bitchiness".

Women who imitate men do not change men's perceptions of them, and clearly intimidation is no longer working for anyone—men or women.

We believe that women have a considerable advantage in a world where the culture of management is being forced to change. Women are by nature more suited to a management style that has been identified by successful CEO's like Sam Walton, and management theorists like Tom Peters as transformational, interactional, developmental, and collaborative. The supportive voice will be more effective and productive than the voice of intimidation in managing a diverse Workforce 2000.

Women have always understood process, and process is an important component of supportive management. The end does not always justify the means, especially when workteams have to continue working and retraining together over time. When workteams are seen as groups of people with needs, ideas, aspirations, skills, and potential the focus changes. Winning the point is no longer the only goal worth pursuing. Realizing mutual interests proves more productive.

Women bring to the workplace a potential to redefine power, effectiveness, and rewards. Their communication styles and relational abilities are clearly suited to supportive management. Culturally, women have grown up with the value that success in life is tied to successful relationships—with friends, with co-workers, with subordinates, with husbands, children, and parents. Whole lifetimes have been spent learning to be effective in these areas. In a workplace where shared power, interaction, team building, and conflict resolution will be the measure, the relational strengths of women will serve to invigorate business strategy and decision making.

Unfortunately, this is easier to articulate than to activate. While it is true that women, because of their sheer numbers, their determination and their cultural orientation have become a force with whom those in power must reckon, it is equally true that those in power are not very anxious to move over to make room at the table. Women may be proving themselves suited for the managerial tasks, but they are still not moving into the managerial ranks in any great numbers. Subtle and not-so-subtle attacks, distortions, discriminatory practices and willful refusal are all workplace stresses with which women continue to struggle. Women are often held more accountable for the very same behavior freely displayed by men. Their reputations in the workplace and their actions are often more vulnerable as well.

Oren Harari, a professor at the University of San Francisco and a consultant with Tom Peters Group, recently made an interesting behavioral perception comparison of men and women in workplace situations. Here is a paraphrased version of some of his observations that appeared in the March 1992 issue of *Management Review*:

* He's agressive. She's pushy.
* He's good at detail. She's picky.
* He's blunt. She's bitchy.
* He's closed-mouthed. She's secretive.
* He's flexible. She's indecisive.
* He's getting married and therefore getting settled. She's getting married and therefore going to get pregnant.
* He's leaving because he sees opportunities. She's leaving because she's undependable.
* He's having lunch with the boss because they're solving problems. She's having lunch with the boss because they're having an affair.
* He's a tough taskmaster. She's hard to work for.

This book is about recognizing obstacles to women's success and fulfillment in the workplace, evaluating them, and making personal choices about what to do.

Strong, successful, and happy women practice various approaches. This book describes what they've done and encourages you to pick and choose the solutions, approaches, and tactics that best apply to your own situation.

*   *   *

This book has been written as a guidebook for a journey—a journey through the workplace of the last decade of the twentieth century.

Five themes emerged from the discussions with our interviewees and they form the backbone of this book. Over and over again women and men pointed out, expanded on, and struggled with these five themes. Here is what they have identified as the major gender challenges for the twenty-first century:

* **The workplace is still a man's world.** This is not because men are better, smarter, stronger, or more entitled, but simply because they are the ones who created it, and they are the ones who still hold the position at the top.
* **The male ego is less formidable than was thought and the female ego is more resourceful than was anticipated.** Women tend to underestimate their ability to deal directly with the male ego.
* **Women and men are different.** These differences will continue to fuel interpersonal difficulties in the workplace. Each believes that if the other would only change his or her behavior the workplace would be less stressful.
* **The workplace will never be sexually neutral.** Sex will always be a factor in the highly charged and competitive atmosphere of business.
* **Women's collaborative, cooperative managerial style has begun to ease out the male model of power and control.** That is the good news. The bad news is that female styles are rewarded as males adopt them, then men move up the corporate ladder faster than women.

This is not a "how-to" book. It is more concerned with "how come?" How did we ever get stuck and how can we move forward. We've looked at concepts like power—its uses and abuses, at politics, and at discrimination in all its overt and covert forms in the workplace.

We have looked at simple things. Things like touching. Touching is often used to maintain a sense of power and control. Think about it. Think about your own experience. Bosses, those in power, feel much freer to touch their subordinates than most subordinates do to touch their bosses. The implications of this observation alone are endless.

You won't find gimmicks between these covers. You won't

learn about how to manipulate your boss or your co-workers, how to change your image, or how to become more assertive. There are many excellent books already in print that will tell you how to do all these things.

Instead, we hope to provide women with some insight on how to take better care of themselves. We share with you what other women in the workforce have to say about emotions, conflict resolution, organizational politics, teamwork, confrontation, cooperation, developing others, and sexual harassment. The goal is not mere survival–it is about making affirmative choices and moving forward. We will show you how other women have used their inner strengths and resisted the ongoing temptation to doubt themselves. Some even had a little fun along the way!

How women handle themselves and capitalize on their strengths makes all the difference in their working lives. The key to surviving and thriving is what it always has been–belief in one's own competence. Competence raises self-esteem. There are no shortcuts. Confronting the male ego, speaking up, realizing your worth, playing from positions of strength, doing the homework, being prepared, conquering ourselves, and separating business from personal issues are steps on the path to professional growth and fulfillment.

Come along with us as we beat a path through the workplace jungle. Through the multiple voices of women who shared their experiences with us, you will find that you are not different, you are not crazy, and you certainly are not alone.

3

Men and Women Are Different

*"The basic discovery about any people is the discovery
of the relationship between its men and its women."*
Pearl Buck

*R*onnie Shippman, a professional golfer, has an interesting
perspective about the differences between men and
women.

"It's been my experience," she says, "that men have a harder
time with disappointment and broken dreams than women
have. They take a longer time to recover from loss and they
feel very sorry for themselves.

"Have you ever watched men watching sports on TV?" she
asked us. "Most sports fans played these games as children
and young men. Most had dreams of being big sports heroes
and superstars. So what do they do when they watch the
games on TV? They scream at the players. They say they could
have done better. They yell that the players, the coaches, and
the managers are stupid and incompetent.

"Now think about a group of women watching ice skating,
ballet, or modern dance on television. Many women wanted to
be ballerinas, actresses, singers, and ice skaters when they

were growing up. We had dreams, too. Do we scream at the ballerinas and say we could do a better job? Do we yell that the dancers are awkward and slow moving? I've never seen it. Women, it seems to me, have always adjusted to reality better than men."

Gary Jeffries, an investment banker, disagrees. He thinks the major difference between men and women is that women talk too much. "Men," he says, "are afraid that women can't keep a confidence. That is devastating in business. We watch women talk all the time and tell each other intimate secrets—we even think, at least *I* think, that women reveal their men's secrets as well.

"If women want to compete with me," he says, "and share the burdens of the workplace as colleagues and partners, they will have to accept the male standard of confidentiality. What I mean by that is I personally will take the risk with a woman colleague if I know that she can keep a confidence. But, if I ever get even a hint there has been a breech of trust, or if I find she has broken a confidence, I'll flatly refuse to work with her again.

"I know another man understands the importance of this kind of trust, but I'm still not sure just what I can expect from a woman."

Problem solving

Estelle Dumont is a tax attorney who says that the law is a rough business. Partners are always stealing the credit from associates and associates steal credit from junior associates. It's an unpleasant fact of life.

"When I was a junior associate," she says, "one of the associates stole some of my work. I suppressed my anger. I chalked it up to his being an asshole, and just made a mental note to be more careful next time.

"When this same associate did it to a male junior associate who worked with me, he went to the partner. He complained to the partner the very FIRST time it happened to him. That's the difference between men and women right there.

"I assumed nothing would happen if I complained. I figured I'd be told he didn't mean it or I was mistaken in some way. The male filed a formal grievance right away and his complaint was taken seriously. He expected it would be. The associate never did it to him again."

Women who experience negative interactions with men in the workplace often feel the one–two punch of being wronged and feeling hopeless about achieving justice. Those of us who attempt to get our own justice sometimes find ourselves applying old remedies to new problems. We ask for rescue from the more powerful, we refuse to "make a scene," and we insist on being reasonable. We feed the problem when we do these things. We must learn to take better care of ourselves than Estelle did.

What was different about the way Estelle's colleague handled this problem from the way Gail, in Chapter 1, the ambulatory director with the telephone-throwing boss, handled hers? Not much. Both went over their supervisor's heads, but the male junior associate solved his problem while Gail felt humiliated and looked for another job.

The expectations of each of the women about the formal "system" ever working for them was very low. Gail assumed "going over her boss's head was terminal." She had no faith in the formal grievance procedure in her organization. Estelle also assumed "nothing would happen if I complained." She believed she would be told she was mistaken or she somehow didn't understand or appreciate the situation.

Estelle's male colleague was not burdened by any of these assumptions. He cut right to the chase. He filed a formal grievance and went to the partner in an open, but no less irate way than Gail approached her supervisor's boss.

The difference lay in the level of exposure he created and in his own level of confidence. He fully expected his grievance to be addressed and that he would be able to move on with his work.

Estelle knows exactly what to do next time, but what might Gail have done differently?

Gail tried to solve her problem too personally and too quietly. She relied on the reasonableness of her supervisor's boss. Her supervisor committed a violent act that frightened not only Gail, but two other employees, yet his boss interpreted this behavior as "overzealous," the reaction of a good, hardworking man under pressure. In his opinion Gail was the one who overreacted.

Had Gail filed a formal grievance, alerted the chief operating officer that she was taking that step, and told her boss she was ready to retain a lawyer to defend her should the grievance procedure fail her, she would have been in a much stronger position.

Gail's formal grievance would have passed over a number of desks in the organization and not everyone who read her charge would interpret Gail's supervisor as a go-getter. The more public her complaint, and the more Gail clearly stated her willingness to pursue a solution beyond the internal channels, the greater her chances would have been for a quick response. While her relationship with Ken would never be pleasant, she would have made it clear to him that his violent temper displays would not be tolerated. In the end she would have kept her job and her ability to make a choice about leaving or staying in a less pressured way.

What women lose when they try to create change, stop abuse, or address harassment without "causing trouble" is respect. Male colleagues respect each other because they know exactly how far they can go before they will experience resistance or revolt. When women draw clear boundaries and stick to them, coping with the male ego in the workplace is less exhausting.

Gail's supervisor's boss could not help her because he did not see anything wrong with Ken's behavior. To have such a driven supervisor in his employ was more positive than negative in his eyes. Gail needed to make a fuss—even though she had been raised not to. Next time, she will take her grievance out of the ego arena and process it through a formal system where people are paid to investigate internal claims of harassment, abuse, and inequitable treatment. Their conclusions about Ken's behavior might have been very different from Dan Mohr's.

Respect and Cooperation

Charles was the older of two boys reared in a loving family with strict adherence to male dominance. There was a big premium on many traits–rationality over feeling, maintaining control, hiding pain, demonstrating physical strength, exerting/articulating superiority over women. Indeed, his father intoned in the midst of any dispute that in his family there could only be one head, the father. Charles observed his family interaction closely and identified strongly with his father. His mother would handle any disagreement with the father, absent of the children, who sometimes prevailed on her to influence the father to soften his position. She chose to facilitate for Charles a closer relationship with the father than with her because she felt Charles would learn more about being an independent, responsible male from his father.

When Charles reached his mid-twenties he understood and revered his father. His mother, whom he loved dearly for her support and kindness, was more of a mystery to him. She had rarely shared with him her opinions or feelings about how to make decisions about conducting one's life. She had consistently deferred to the father on these matters. In turn, Charles had paid little attention to the complexities or subtleties of his mother's life. He depended on her to take care of him and to anticipate his needs. He never considered how she negotiated her needs or problem solved. For him, it was his father who made all things possible and it was like his father–cool, reasoned, and self-assured that he aspired to be.

Charles worked in an engineering firm that was historically a male preserve. The organization was managed for control and compliance and Charles thought he would be right at home. Women had just begun to enter his industry, an event that meant the company now had to include women's lounges and change the concept of the engineers' lounge to a men's room and a women's room.

He had learned in college that women were often smarter than he, and he had been impressed by the competitive adroitness and competence of many of his female peers. He was in awe of this discovery and wondered how he was supposed to behave when one of these super-brains was his boss. He was spurred by the notion that it was highly probable he would run a company one day . . . an expectation no woman could realistically entertain.

When Charles was assigned to a team project that reported to a senior engineer, he was very pleased. He felt apprehensive when he learned his boss would be a woman, "someone named Rose."

Rose had grown up in a male-dominated household and was comfortable working with groups of men. She was familiar with their approach to problem solving and their use of competition as a means of male bonding. Sometimes they used the process of work as the vehicle to compete with and position themselves with each other. She knew from her brothers that the world of business, just like the football field, was a proving ground for men where they outdid each other and tried to perform as heroes in front of women.

Rose and Charles had two distinct points of view and a different set of values. They had different rules for playing the same game. Charles viewed the game as more important than the people. She viewed each participant as more important than the game.

She had to forge a team of this group of men and they had to see her as its captain. Fortunately, this new team had two members with whom she had worked successfully on another project. She knew she could count on them to help orient the others. Indeed, sometimes she made sure one or two of the men on her projects understood its goals and her approach prior to the first group meeting so they could interpret her expectations to the others.

She had learned long ago that some men do not even *hear* what is said if the direction comes from a woman. Thus, she would co-opt a few of their peers as a strategy to get herself heard.

She also had learned from experience that she had to be overly prepared. Whereas men are often given the benefit of the doubt, some men assume that a woman does not know what she is doing. Being unprepared and unable to handle a challenge puts a woman at a decided disadvantage. Now the minute she was challenged or treated in some gratuitous, gender-specific way she dealt with it immediately. She *never* acted flustered.

Rose began her meeting with the project team by outlining the commitments the company had made to the client. Her presentation was clear, included all the background analysis, and anticipated numerous problems. Her style had matured into confident, friendly, firm, and assertive from the start. She had worked hard to overcome an earlier tendency to be really nice or accommodating.

Charles decided he was not going to take Rose seriously. When she finished the overview of the project he said, "Whatever you want to do, doll."

The other men bristled at Charles or sneered at Rose. Without missing a beat, Rose said, "Well, honey, I'm glad to see you are so cooperative. We have all day to work through the ways each of you will work on this assignment. Charles, I want you to think of three ways your talents can advance this project."

Charles retreated and Rose continued with her process. In so doing, she let the men know she was not going to fall prey to their power game. She was not derailed by this nonsubstantive challenge. She challenged Charles to cooperate.

Rose set up ground rules for their working and communicating together. Each person's contribution would be valued, each had to listen to the other without interruption. Client differences would be negotiated based on mutual gains to all parties. They were to avoid treating those with opposing views like the enemy. This strategy was to get them to communicate with each other. This was a complex project that required a high level of collaboration. Their tendency was to assign each person a specific task and to go off and complete it with little interaction with each other. If something went wrong, they would blame someone other than themselves. She paired them in various work assignments so that they would have individual tasks and group tasks. This was how she facilitated their working together.

Rose's collaborative, cooperative management style over-rode the male model of power and control.

Charles learned how to work cooperatively in the work setting and that there were other modes of achieving one's goal.

Sometimes he wondered if the world of work had experienced a sea change from his father's day, and often he felt confused. It was a discussion he thought he should have with his mother.

Gender Roles

From birth, men and women are socialized to enact specific gender roles. In our culture, men are ascribed a dominant role to the females' subordinate position. This difference is recognized by men and women as male control and independence; female inequality and dependence.

Culture defines the kinds of behavioral scripts that males and females are molded to perform. For example, boys don't cry no matter how much hurt or pain they may be enduring, girls speak in ladylike tones even if no one can hear them, girls are taught to understand feelings and emotions, boys are taught to think and be rational, girls lead with their hearts, boys lead with their heads. Boys learn competitive sports and to compete with each other, girls learn to cooperate and to take care of others in their play. Boys learn early the rudiments of controlling and suppressing their emotions. Girls learn emotional expressiveness.

Pauline Lee is an elementary school teacher who told us that distinct patterns are already evident in male and female children's behavior by the time they start school.

"In my experience," she says, "parents expect girls to be responsible by the time they reach school age. The majority of the girls in my class already fulfill that expectation. They behave, they do their homework, and seldom involve their parents with problems they experience at school.

"Most of the notes I get asking that a child be excused from not completing homework or for missing a test come from mothers of boys. I once got a letter from a mother asking me to forgive her son for not being able to do his work! It's my belief that these repeated requests for special treatment and for permission to be exempted from responsibility can't help but feed a sense of entitlement, even at such an early age.

"Mothers have come to school asking me to review with them and with their son why a certain answer was marked wrong on a test. They take time off from their jobs to do this.

"Girls are told to 'go ask the teacher why she marked you wrong on that answer.' In other words, they are expected to take care of solving such problems on their own. And they do. The result is that developmentally girls move ahead faster in the early grades than boys do. It is not until puberty that this pattern begins to reverse itself.

"Girls feel a strong desire to please their parents by being good, taking care of their responsibilities, and not causing a fuss." Pauline says, "On the other hand, boys feel freer to be less responsible, less attentive and less well behaved because an expectation that they will control themselves and feel responsible for their effect on other people has not been placed on them."

During the formative years, mothers typically are the care-taker for boys and girls. To establish one's sexual identity, one needs to identify with the parent of the same sex. Boys have to eventually break the connection with their mothers. Girls remain connected to their mothers who see them as exten-sions of themselves. Mothers' experience their sons as differ-ent. Men carry their ambivalence about this disruptive process throughout their lives.

The Workplace

In the workplace, men maintain their disconnection through the dynamics of indifference, power, exclusivity, competitiveness, aggression, and objectivity, all of which characterize a man's pattern of interaction. His usual communication style is intellectual or physical.

When men make decisions in the men's room, turn the conversation to athletic teams, pass around a piece of paper with a "for males' eyes only joke" they are practicing exclusion. Remember Cindy's experience.

When they try to undermine your effectiveness, steal your ideas, whisper or shout that they can do the job better, nitpick your data, ask yourself, "Is he being competitive?"

If the issue being discussed is framed to separate people from problems and focus on logical reasons or the principle of the matter, then they are operating objectively.

Although maleness portends a life of dominance combined with a sense of entitlement based on gender, the return is the societal expectation that men will work and provide economic support to the family. Aaron French is thirteen years old. Aaron believes that people are always ready to excuse girls when they mess up but no one–especially his parents or his teachers–are so ready to defend him. "Girls have it easy," he says. "People expect too much of boys."

Boys are supposed to develop competence and to achieve. Families and schools lay the groundwork for this role expectation. As an adult, competence at work and earning power become central factors of a man's life. What he does in his role as breadwinner defines who and what he is.

The Female Ego

The female ego is organized around caring for others, inclusiveness, nurturance, and connecting with others via relationships. Being aware of the emotional content of an exchange, being generous with time, concern for others, empathy and cooperation are characteristics that shape female development. In the workplace, women act within the context of relatedness and interconnection with others. Women like to talk things out, fix problems, make sure everyone's interests are met, preserve harmony, and affect mutual empowerment.

In the past, most women had to depend on men for their economic support and survival. Many women, however, especially less economically privileged women, have always worked and contributed to their own or their family's survival. There is much to be learned from their experience. Now, many more women, as a class, face the necessity of performing competently in the workplace to earn wages to support themselves, their children, or their family's life goals. Women and men are beginning to relinquish the passing cultural imperatives: women are dependent on men for total financial support and men rule the family. We are seeing the beginnings of an interdependency. However, women still compete in an environment where her career is seen as ancillary or less important than a man's.

In our society issues of race and class intersect with gender roles to complicate the equation and to determine an upperclass, white male standard of behavior in the workplace. For those excluded from this category, minorities, women, and less advantaged white men, the world of work can be a place where there are barriers to success as well as attitudes that they are expected to fail or perform less well. Women and minorities are rarely given full credit for outstanding abilities unless, like a sports star, it is impossible to deny performance carried out before one's eyes.

The Future

In the next century, we expect to see tables of organization flatten and managerial positions disappear. Companies will use quality circles, task groups, and non-hierarchal cross-disciplinary project teams to do a task. Interpersonal skills will determine success as team building and cross-functional matrixes replace the traditional business hierarchy.

There is currently a quiet evolution rather than an obvious revolution. Collaboration, flexibility, consensus, and participation are practiced arts of interpersonal communication and emerge from concern for others. Men and women will need these skills to improve productivity in and to negotiate the workplace.

Stu Reed is a surgeon who played team sports throughout his youth and in college. "In medicine we are put in situations where we have to work as teams. Everybody has a job to do and if one person screws up, your whole team fails. Varsity sports helped prepare me for this. In my era, women did not have that opportunity. Now my daughters play basketball and hockey. They are growing in self-confidence. They are learning team play and how to handle wins and losses. My kids don't take the losses personally and look forward to getting on the court again. Every game is a new challenge."

Brad Fisher thinks that women bring to the workplace an ability to be more responsible and to hear and look at many sides of an issue. "They listen more carefully. Women have played the major role in socializing us and that has given them a broader perspective and an ability to respond to a broader view."

Men and women are different. There is an undertow below the surface of their interaction. Distinguishing between the subcurrents of sex and power is essential for women so that they do not get their responses confused.

Women have experienced the difference in many ways. Sometimes they work too hard and overextend themselves (give too much),*i.e.*, more than their male colleagues to help out, advance their careers, or be cooperative. They learn the hard way that their efforts are not always rewarded. Often they are seen and not heard. Always, they have to be ready to navigate the sexual terrain. Increasingly, they are learning how to transform what could be scenarios of unbridgeable difference to their advantage.

Expectations

Colleen Daly is head nurse of a surgical unit at a specialty hospital. She remembers a situation that occurred while she was a nursing student—one she says still bothers her today. "One of the physicians in the hospital where I did my training was a retina specialist," she says. "He had a big private practice and when his surgical technician, David, left he asked if I could do some patient testing on a freelance basis until he could hire a full-time employee. I agreed to do it for him.

I discovered that David had been scheduling ten patients a day for testing. I found I could do more and soon I was scheduling twenty appointments on the days I worked. Then the doctor asked me if it was possible to schedule more than twenty. I felt kind of hurt when he asked, after all he was paying me less than half the rate he had paid David, but I reminded myself that I was doing this as a quasi-favor–whatever that is. I said I'd try.

"Next, I began to find more and different kinds of work left for me to do. First it was mail to sort and answer. Then, forms to be filled out and filed with the insurance companies. And never a word of thanks or even acknowledgment that virtually from day one I had doubled the number of patients he was able to see. I didn't know what to do.

"First, I told a friend that I had assumed this doctor and I were not only colleagues but friends. I thought we were doing each other a favor–for me, a few extra bucks, for him, some help until he could make a new hire. I felt used and stupid. I told her that I couldn't do it any longer. I was going to leave and not tell him why. My friend suggested a better approach–confront him! I met with David and shared my concern. He told me he thought I was willing to do more since I never complained. I asked for a raise and did better than I expected. We negotiated my getting a percentage of what I generated for the business."

Leverage

Roberta Maxwell is a chemistry professor. She says that within four months of joining the faculty of a large Midwestern university she was given fourteen committee assignments. By contrast, her less-experienced male counterpart, who had no laboratory to run, no committee assignments, was given an opportunity to run a program. "In retrospect," she says, "I think it reflected my being female, black, and having years of administrative experience. They knew I wanted to succeed and they knew I could get things done.

"At about six months into my tenure I passed one of the deans in the hall. He complimented me on doing such a fine job. 'But why are you doing your dean's work?' he laughed. 'He makes $20,000 more than you. He should be doing what he has you doing on all those committees.'

"It took me two weeks to submit my reports to the dean and resign from two-thirds of the committees. But not before I realized my ambition had led me to be used as a token. I was furious. Tokenism is a problem when you are one of a few among many and the employer wants to show diversity in the faculty or workforce. Then you are trotted out for everything. I have always felt the pressure to be a credit to women and blacks. I went to the dean. I knew I had everything to gain. I told him I was now well informed about the university, our department, and its problems. I wanted him to know I knew where some of the skeletons were buried and where he might be vulnerable. He was somewhat horrified, but he acknowledged I had done a great job. I wanted to run a program, so I used this opportunity to ask for what I wanted. After some struggle, I managed to get exactly what I wanted."

Turning the Tables

There are more women in the workforce now than ever before, yet we still do not have the respect and earnings that men have.

Hazel Carter, an executive vice president, says, "We have a board that is made up of men who went to college together. They usually start talking about their last golf game or their college basketball days. They always try to outdo the other. They focus on what is part of them . . . what they have shared or what is historical. Subjects that clearly exclude women.

"I walk into the board room. They all look at me. They make an off-color joke. Then they look at me again. They make a comment or laugh, then they look at me again. I don't know where they learned this behavior. They have an inability to treat me the same way they treat each other.

"I noticed this behavior is usually pitched to the man with the highest prestige or the most senior person. Before the next meeting I read each board member's biography and press clippings to ascertain what else interested them, especially the senior person. At the next meeting, I turned the conversation to his interest and engaged him, for instance, in a discussion about opera. This gave the others an experience of being ignored or remotely interested in a subject."

Sharon Ford articulates what women have heard repeatedly. "Women are perceived as strident if they are aggressive about their points of view. If she interrupts, she is rude. If she is tough, objective, or rational, she is acting like a man. When she presents the analytic data well, she is thinking like a man. Women in business make a mistake by focusing so much on gender. You are going to be perceived in various ways over which you have little control. Wear your purple suit, wear the latest fashions. Who cares as long as you are competent. A good approach is to think about the task and not get hung up on the prejudices about women. If you are batting your eyes make sure you are not missing a line of the balance sheet."

Joyce Lorenzo is a plumbing contractor. "There are some definite advantages to being a woman in a male environment," Joyce says. "It's an advantage to know that most men you run into cannot escape their view of females as sex objects. You can look at that as a negative or a positive. I choose to see it as a positive.

"What do I care if a rival is looking at my legs instead of listening to me? He loses his concentration and I win the contract.

"If a man reacts to me in a gender-specific way it means he is going to underestimate me. I consider it to my advantage. It means he is going to engage in predictable behavior. I win because he is a prisoner of his own preconceptions."

In the workplace we strive for parity of opportunity, pay, achievement, and creativity. Being in a subordinate position works against that. Coping with the male ego in the workplace means we must recognize by sight, or some other sense, the undertow, disarm it, and make it friendly. We have to be seen *and* heard.

Conclusion

In her groundbreaking book, *You Just Don't Understand*, Deborah Tannen observes that, "Boys and girls grow up in different worlds, but we think we're in the same one, so we judge each other's behavior by the standards of our own."

We solve our problems in different ways, have different expectations and operate in the workplace with different definitions of power, ambition, and success. Because the communication styles of men and women are so different, we are often at odds with each other in the workplace.

As women climb the hierarchical ladder, we find ourselves functioning in an environment where procedures, behaviors, strategies, and politics discredit most of the values we were taught as children. If we want to stay there we must find ways to adapt our own behaviors and cope with the behaviors of our male colleagues.

Men are just beginning to learn how to compete with women. They have spent their lives competing with each other–learning to be aggressive, to take risks, to think and act logically, and to defend "the rules." Men know what to expect from other men. Competition *is* their relationship.

Competing with women in the workplace, however, is a challenge for men. Competing *for* women, in sexual ways, is familiar, but competing *with* them professionally for positions, resources, and influence is something very different. Old behaviors sometimes get in the way as men struggle to interact with these women who are not their mothers, sisters, girlfriends, or daughters.

4

Obstacles to Women in the Workplace

"The thing women must do to rise to power is to redefine their femininity. Once power was considered a masculine attribute. In fact, power has no sex."
                                        Katherine Graham

*B*ill Deerfield is the bursar of a small women's college. Bill is hated by his colleagues because he gets into everyone's business and refuses to provide any real help.

"Bill is a dinosaur," says Pam Friedman, the development officer. It's doubly frustrating because the president of the college supports Bill's position on every issue no matter how ridiculous.

When he was confronted by the senior staff, the president told them to "Do the best you can. Bill takes his fiscal responsibilities very seriously . . . he'll be retiring soon anyway."

Soon, however, was not soon enough. Bill blocked a proposal to allow tuition to be paid with credit cards, and he stubbornly insisted that the payroll system stand alone and not be interactive with personnel. The president supported him on both issues.

"Bill is going to move us back into the nineteenth century and straight into bankruptcy court," complained the distressed controller.

"Bill's just being cautious," the president explained, "somebody around here has to be . . . ."

Bill's mean-spirited interference made the provost so angry she vowed to find "the" issue that would "get" Bill. She suspected that since he was so intent on minding everyone else's business he might have slipped somewhere in conducting his own.

When she found it, she was overjoyed. It seemed that Bill refused to permit the non-tenure track staff (the lecturers) to be classified as regular staff. He instructed the personnel director, over the objection of the provost (yet fully supported by the president), to classify the group as "independent contractors."

This meant they would have to arrange to pay their own payroll taxes and would not be eligible to receive benefits. Bill thought this would save the college money.

An IRS audit found the college liable for four years back payroll tax for fifty lecturers and imposed an additional $100,000 fine.

The provost could hardly contain her joy. Surely this exposure would force the president to put Bill on a shorter leash! Fair is fair . . . .

On her way to the president's office she shared her treasure with the development officer.

"You must be nuts," Pam responded. "This will be covered up and everything will be status quo."

The provost was shocked. "Don't you know about Bill?" Pam asked. "Didn't anyone ever tell you? Bill is an investment genius. That's his claim to fame. In addition to getting a nice piece of change for the college, he's been investing funds for the trustees. He keeps them very happy and they're all very interested in keeping him happy.

"Our dear president knows that if it came to a choice between himself and Bill, he'd be out of a job. My dear," continued Pam sadly, "you have nothing. If you want to win points with the president, think of a way to solve this quietly and keep Bill's name out of it."

The provost finally understood the priorities at her institution. Politics clearly ranked above progress, customer service, and good sense.

Organizational Politics

Two powerful obstacles women struggle with in the workplace every day are organizational politics and organizational politicians. What and who are they?

Management textbooks tell us that every organization creates formal systems that are accepted ways of doing business. These formal systems are documented in the firm's policy manuals, regulatory, and procedure books. Unfortunately, they usually bear little resemblance to the ways in which the work actually gets done.

Organizational politics deal with the "secret" ways these policies, regulations, and procedures are ignored, subverted, and avoided. This takes some skill and influence. Enter the organizational politician. A newcomer can figure some of it out–but not all. Someone must guide you through organizational politics. It differs from firm to firm. Organizational politics means the "way we do it here." To learn these lessons well you need a tutor.

Men take care of this aspect of their education by finding a mentor and by getting accepted into the inside circle of organizational politicians. An invitation is, however, usually required. It's estimated that 75 percent of executives who are forced out of their positions–males and females–lose their jobs because of organizational politics. The informal system can either help or hurt your chances of succeeding in an organization.

Executives who lose their jobs often are neither incapable nor incompetent; they simply miss cues, clues, and opportunities. They are people who were manipulated and/or maneuvered in some way out of position and finally out of power–victims of skilled organizational politicians who may even have been less capable than they were! It is a fact of organizational life that in some situations it matters less how good you are than how well you perform in the game of organizational politics.

Organizational politics flow through informal channels and networks. Subsystems are formed to move recommendations, policies, and people more easily and quickly than it would be to accomplish the same goals through the formal system. These networks, although informal, are very powerful.

The "hidden" structure of an organization has tremendous influence on the way the goals of the organization are achieved. Those who are welcomed into the Informal Network are "groomed" for promotion through the hierarchy. They are "sponsored" by mentors and given access to information and to those who can get them the things they need as they move ahead. A 1986 study by Korn/Ferry International revealed that the corporate leaders they surveyed rated mentoring second only to education as having had a significant impact on their success.

Although all of this may sound very mysterious, it really isn't so difficult to understand or to observe in an organization. A new employee is usually welcomed into the network when he or she is seen as a "good fit" with the group. A good fit, however, has traditionally meant white male. Since networks are usually set up by men, men are usually their first choice.

Social scientists tell us that people tend to move toward those who share their characteristics and away from those who are different. A homogenous group feels safe. Members feel comfortable with each other and trust each other. They know what to expect. Cohesiveness is very important when the stakes are high and when risky and difficult decisions must be made.

When a change, such as admitting women into the circle, is introduced, the trust level decreases. The group can become unstable and the ability to make decisions and arrive at consensus is affected. This is one reason "newcomers" who don't fit the profile often remain outside the network–sometimes clearly and visibly ignored.

Take the case of Celeste Albright who was one of two interns accepted by a prestigious law firm for training. Harris Black was the other. "The partner we were assigned to didn't know what to do with me," Celeste says. "That was evident to Harry and me right from the beginning. He found something wrong with every brief I wrote–everything he got from Harry, on the other hand, was brilliant.

"He took Harry to lunch with him and left me at the office. Harry went to collective bargaining sessions and I was excluded. He told me I'd never be called on to 'work a session' and Harry would–it was 'backroom practice' and he wanted to show Harry the ropes. I took it, but I was angry.

"Finally, though, I just had to know if it was me. I asked Harry if just once he'd switch work with me and submit my brief as his and his as mine. Harry was a good guy and I guess at some level he was curious too. He agreed to do it.

"Sure enough. Harry's presentation (which I wrote) was brilliant, and 'mine' was food for the dog. At least I knew it wasn't me. But you know," says Celeste, "this could have been devastating to my career. Someone else might have given up at this point. He could have convinced me that I would never make it in a field I'm excelling in right now. I never confronted the partner with what I knew. I just moved on. But I never forgot."

Celeste had not been invited into the inner circle. Harry had.

Getting into the Informal Circle

Hilda Rivera is a scientist. When she began her new job at a research institution she was the only woman in the department. "When I arrived," she says, "departmental meetings were not regularly scheduled. My colleagues made decisions on their way back from the men's room or at lunch. Decisions were made in arenas where I was excluded. They would meet informally and then say to me, 'Oh, we thought you knew about the meeting.' I dealt with this by asking the dean to schedule meetings and to let me know in advance when they were scheduled. Nobody was happy about it initially, but they did it. And now it's working fine."

Getting into the informal ranks is not easy. You cannot win a place for yourself through hard work. Doing more than your colleagues generally does not impress them.

One ticket in is having, or having access to, something that represents value to the members. Networks are built on a set of mutual obligations, loyalty to colleagues who can help or hurt, and lots of information exchange. If you are in control of valuable resources, or if you have expertise in an area that can be helpful, or know "outside people" you can connect others with, make it known. If you have access to information with limited distribution—or even if you can potentially cause trouble—make sure you make that public too.

Hilda Rivera says that the chairman's ability to get her to sign a contract was a feather in his cap. "Scientists are a pretty independent bunch," she says. "My leverage has always been that I bring in more money than anyone else in my department. Money talks. I have other problems now. I've come to be viewed as a threat. But I do manage to get the information that I need."

Getting into the informal circle often depends on the support a woman gets from her boss. A powerful boss can either facilitate or block her entry.

Because a supportive boss is key to entry into the informal circle, it is important to make yourself invaluable to your boss. Loyalty and competence count. Loyalty is a trait that always appears at the top of the list of characteristics that executives value and reward in their subordinates.

Work consistently at establishing your credibility and trustworthiness. Employees who develop a reputation for integrity and good interpersonal communication are attractive to the powerful. They possess traits that are helpful to the policymakers and operators of any organization.

"It's so important to have your boss's support," says Lynne Aldridge, a marketing executive, "because he or she can sponsor you. It's so frustrating to feel like you are on the team but not in the game. That's just what it's like when you're locked outside the informal circle where all the real action takes place."

Forming Alliances

The intensity of organizational politics ebbs and flows in any organization. When a firm is undergoing change, or when the institution's goals are vague, or when resources become limited politicians start coming out of the woodwork. Any situation that threatens the status of the powerful people in your organization, or has the potential to allow others to grab a share of power, is a situation you should pay close attention to.

Why? Because under such conditions the decisions that get made, decisions that can affect you, are made for political instead of practical or rational reasons. Sometimes the best you can do under these conditions is to protect yourself. And you can't protect yourself unless you have taken the time to form alliances.

Allies can protect you through their position in the organization or by their knowledge of what's coming. Make your alliances in high places if you can. Like Hilda, learn to control your information and influence carefully. Make sure those you have helped in the past know they owe you a favor and that you fully expect to collect someday.

Lauretta Scott, a chemical engineer, encourages women to build alliances. "You have to have information," she says. "Men are constantly trading information. You have to become part of the information exchange. You have to know something before someone else. If people don't think you are in the loop, then you are not seen as useful to them."

If it's possible, try to get an early success in your organization–and make it public. This will make you a desirable ally. And finally, don't get embroiled in petty disputes. Save your favors, your alliances, and your information for the big time. If you can't get free from a dispute, however, finish it. See it through to resolution and don't let it fester.

"A wounded animal is more deadly than an angry one," says Pam Denby, managing editor of a trade magazine. "It is always better to make peace early, but if that's not possible, finish your rival off. If you don't, you will deal with him (or her) for the rest of your stay with the organization."

Networking

It's important to develop expertise in politics. It's important to learn to influence and to persuade. This is the foundation for building power in an organization. Creating your own coalitions and networks also helps.

"Until women fill the executive ranks in organizations in greater numbers the primary vehicle for women helping women will be networking," says Pam. "There are simply not enough senior-level female mentors to go around. Men mentoring women is encouraged in forward-looking companies, but as an ongoing practice it is relatively rare."

Three networking activities crucial to career success are: participation in the invisible network within your own organization; creation of your own internal network to share information and strategies with trusted associates; and participation in professional trade organizations and associations with others in your field.

The first activity ties you into the communication system that enables you to get things done at your home base. The others help you develop confidence in yourself as you flex your professional muscles. They are support systems that encourage sharing resources, exchanging information, testing ideas, and developing creative solutions in a safe and enthusiastic atmosphere. If you are lucky enough to have a mentor in addition to these connections, then you are lucky indeed.

Edna Brown, an operations manager, counsels women not to be afraid of networking outside their own areas. "Talk to a more senior staff member about how to deal with something. Seek their advice and maybe you'll learn something. Maybe you'll make some valuable connections. Women should learn to ask. Men do it all the time. Network and mentor.

"Consider calling up the CEO," she says, "just to ask him what he would do in this or that hypothetical situation.

Women have to stop being afraid to ask for information for fear of being perceived as less competent."

"Just getting into the Network is so important," says Anne. "You can't change anything if you can't get inside. Women should not allow themselves to become isolated. And standing outside complaining, bitching that they won't let you in, well, that will set us all back twenty years . . . ."

The Glass Ceiling

The "glass ceiling" is another obstacle women struggle with in the workplace. The United States Department of Labor defines the glass ceiling as an "artificial barrier based on attitudinal or organizational bias that prevents qualified minorities and women from advancing into middle and senior-level management positions."

Like organizational politics, the glass ceiling is invisible. It exists at different levels in different organizations, and the only way you know where it begins is by bumping against it.

The ceiling is a barrier whose foundation is built on the organization's traditions, its management climate, and conscious and unconscious assumptions by those in charge about women's skills, abilities, and expectations. It is the line women will find almost impossible to cross and may be found at either the supervisory, middle management, or executive level. You know where it is in your own organization simply because you can't seem to get beyond it no matter what you do.

The building blocks of the glass ceiling are the notions that women, because of family responsibilities (as if men had none), have less commitment to careers than men; that women are not as skilled at risk taking as men; that women are too emotional and react erratically under pressure.

Victor Castanada, a successful real estate developer with over thirty years in the workforce, observes that when men have to go home early to take care of children they are seen as good family men. If a woman must leave early, it is cited as a reason she is not going to succeed.

"Women ought to confront this bias as directly as possible," he says. "They should ask, 'Do you have a problem with my work? Did I miss a deadline?' The male ego, you see, is not as formidable as women think. The best way to deal with it is to confront it with competence. Women should make sure that their work is on time and is accurate. Then they should demand equal treatment for pulling equal weight."

Sylvia Elgin, a finance manager for a manufacturer of heavy equipment, agrees with Victor and goes a step further. "I think single women are treated differently from both married women and single guys in the workforce. It is clearly expected that single women will show up. The company assumes that you don't have a life of your own. The family in corporate America is the most legitimate out you have for not killing yourself.

"For example, last year we were in Paris at a trade show. My boss had to return home early because he had to go to his daughter's soccer match. The only way he could get back in time was to take the Concorde. So he did. I could never do that because I'm not seen as having a legitimate reason to return in a hurry."

Some organizational cultures reflect the assumption that men are better suited than women for decision making. The model of the successful manager in our society is still macho: aggressive, rational, decisive. It assumes that men do not bring personal problems and emotional baggage to the workplace with them. It assumes there is a woman at home taking care of all those things for him—an archaic assumption in the 1990s.

Victor suggests, "Some assumptions will just have to be taken for what they are initially, until you find yourself in a position where it is possible to change them. For example," he says, "a male junior manager who finds that his boss is domi-nating and controlling has to learn to use that to his own advantage. With women the issue of gender is added to the equation. The American way of business is hierarchical. It is based on control and dominance and you have to learn how to handle it."

Men, especially those who have been in the workforce for twenty years or more, may still feel uncomfortable with the idea of depending on women for business advice, information, and decision making–it feels foreign to them. The idea of taking orders from a woman doesn't feel so good to some either. Did you ever wonder why it's often so difficult for a woman to be "heard" at a meeting?

Breaking Through

Emily Howard is a trustee on the board of her local art museum. She is one of two original female board members in a group of eighteen trustees. "I think that men have trouble accepting the identity of women in all-male conclaves," she says. "The men on my board confused the other female board member with me for years. Her name was Angela. They kept calling me Angela and her Emily–as if we were interchangeable. I guess to them we were."

When Angela left the board another woman took her place. "Then they started calling me by her name. That's when I lost it. It was only after I caused a scene that I became an individual to them. Everybody knows who Emily is now."

Lauretta handled a similar situation in a different way. "I have been in meetings," she says, "where it became obvious to me that people were talking around me, ignoring me. What I did was stop the meeting. When I had everyone's attention I said, 'I know we all want to move this project, but nothing is going to get done unless you begin to deal with me. I am willing to wait.'

"Now I know that's a very aggressive thing to do. But it saved a lot of time. They knew I wasn't going to put up with any nonsense. But you have to be competent in order to get away with being aggressive. Once you throw down the mantle or put out the challenge you have to be prepared to meet it."

Even women sometimes assume that young women will get pregnant and leave the organization, or that they won't move to accept a promotion because they have a husband who also has a career. Women are in a double bind–in addition to being mothers, daughters, wives, and sisters they are also colleagues, competitors, clients–people trying to build careers.

To begin to smash glass ceilings at whatever point they are encountered, women can make sure they let their bosses know what their ambitions are. They can request more important assignments. They can ask to be put on task forces where women have been overlooked in the past.

Anyone can request a career plan review at annual evaluation time. Anyone can apply for training in areas where further development is needed. Every reasonable question that you ask requires an answer. If you are really dealing with a glass ceiling sooner or later those who are defending it will run out of excuses.

Clara Harvey, a corporate travel agent, suggests that women quietly identify a male colleague holding the same level of position they do and who has about the same length of time with the company. "Use him as a benchmark," she said. "Watch his progress and if all else is equal and he begins to pull ahead while you're standing still, ask why. You're entitled to an answer. Sadly, it may be that you were just overlooked, not considered–an oversight. That's okay for now, as long as it gets fixed."

"Women can learn from men to ask, directly and clearly for what they want," says Sylvia. "We've got to take more risks in moving our careers along and in requesting promotions. We've got to stop trying to be such good, hard-working girls hoping that we'll be noticed and rewarded. It just doesn't happen that way. We've got to stop asking for permission and waiting to be discovered."

Sexual Harassment

Sally Stephens is an art director at a large advertising agency. She is an ambitious young woman who hopes one day to be promoted to group head. She works for Gary Best, a creative supervisor who she describes simply as a "bully." Gary tries to keep all his subordinates–men and women–on edge. "The men cope," says Sally, "by trying to imitate Gary's style. The women cope by trying to hang on long enough to get promoted or transferred out of his division."

Sally describes the abuse in Gary's division as "blatant."

When the president of their company released a memo to the staff advising them of the company's policy on sexual harassment everyone howled with laughter. The day before the policy came out, Sally overheard Gary advising one of the supervisors not to promote Sheila Guzman, another art director and a colleague of Sally's. "Don't promote her," Gary said. "She'll only get pregnant." This was just a few months after Sheila had gotten married.

"Everyone was afraid of him," Sally says. "He fired someone just because she was fat. One guy was doing well and he started wearing his hair long. Gary took the first opportunity to fire him for a minor mistake–something that would have been overlooked if someone else had done it. The atmosphere was terrible.

"The worst thing he ever did to me was in the middle of a presentation I was making to clients–one I had worked very hard on. He leaned over and commented on the texture of my panty hose. Nobody else heard him. He whispered, which made it look like he was giving me advice. It completely blew my concentration. I barely recovered my train of thought and didn't look professional at all, even though I had been well prepared. His protégée, whose presentation followed mine, looked very good by comparison."

If politics is the most common obstacle that women face in the workforce then sexual harassment is the most difficult. Four months after the Senate Judiciary Committee's confirmation hearings of Clarence Thomas, Sue Browder wrote in *New Woman* magazine:

> As I talked to dozens of angry women, I realized their rage wasn't really about Anita Hill or Clarence Thomas or who was telling the truth. As the *Los Angeles Times* noted, it was really "about women's feelings of powerlessness and the fundamental differences in the ways men and women experience the world." Most women sided with Hill not because they knew Thomas was lying–many believed the whole truth would never be known–but because they knew what had happened to

them. Studies have shown that anywhere from 42 to 88 percent of women have been sexually harassed.

What is sexual harassment? Federal law divides it into two varieties. The first, *quid pro quo*, occurs when a person in power offers a promotion, or any other kind of financial benefit, to another person with the condition that the receiver provides sexual favors to the giver. This form also includes the subordinate being punished in any way for refusing to submit to the supervisor's sexual advances.

The second kind of sexual harassment is called the "hostile work environment." It exists when either supervisors or colleagues create an atmosphere that is so sexually charged—either by joke telling, unwelcome touching, obscene language—or sabotaging an employee's work to make her look bad—that it affects people's ability to do their work.

Cindy, the copywriter in Chapter 1, who endured the "dumb blonde" jokes over lunch with her boss and her clients experienced a hostile environment.

Cindy felt guilty about freezing in that situation. Should she have walked out? Tried to stop them? Humiliated them in some way? In the end, her need for her paycheck overrode her sense of outrage and she felt defeated. She became angry not only at her boss, but at herself. Cindy is not alone.

Cindy might have asked to be taken off the account. This is why it is so important for women to become excellent at their work. If Cindy had the expertise these clients needed, she would have been in a good position to refuse her services until, and unless, the boss did something about his own behavior and the behavior he encouraged in the clients.

If Cindy was not in such a key position she could still refuse to respond to the situation. She may not have had a choice about the lunch conversation, but she was under no obligation to laugh. There is always hope that one of the "boys" would have felt some sense of shame.

There is never one right way to handle an uncomfortable interaction. Cindy might have communicated her discomfort to her boss when they returned to the office. She could do this without anger or self-righteousness. He might have trivialized her concerns (her own colleague, Jim, was not sympathetic) or he might have reacted with anger or sarcasm, but she would have had the satisfaction of knowing that she had protested in some way. She could have congratulated herself for refusing to slip away feeling victimized. She would also have prevented the anger she ultimately felt at herself.

Sexism vs. Sexual Harassment

Jackie Baldridge, a hospital management consultant, observes that "sexism manifests itself differently in different generations. In the 1990s it's become more subtle–it's gone underground. I deal with comments loaded with sexual innuendo nearly every day," she says. "I see this as an attempt to keep me in my place. Because it is so very subtle I know those who continue to do it know exactly what they're doing."

Sexism is the assumption that men are naturally superior to women. Women who we spoke with at all levels of responsibility and authority in the workforce agree with Jackie. Sexism is not only alive, but it is mutating–becoming more difficult to identify and deal with effectively.

Sexual harassment is a direct result of sexism. Sexual harassment stems from a desire to bully and humiliate women. It is the cruelest practice of the male ego. Women who are attractive are at no more risk for sexual harassment than those who are not so attractive.

The goal clearly is intimidation. Sadly, it works. The emotional turmoil resulting from sexual harassment affects work performance and causes many women to withdraw from the competition.

Marilyn Murdock, in her book, *Powerful Leadership Skills for Women*, defines sexual harassment very clearly. "It is," she says, "any unwanted behavior that interferes with the ability to work in an atmosphere free of intimidation. In its more severe forms it creates an implicit or explicit condition for employment or promotion."

If the definition is so clear, why does so much confusion

surround the problem? One reason is that in sexual harassment, as in all forms of harassment, the boundaries between offensiveness and "kidding" and between the intentional and the unconscious are sometimes blurred.

Wanda works as a switchboard operator for a brokerage house. One of the order clerks started calling her several times a day to tell her obscene jokes and to ask her personal questions. He thought it was funny. When Wanda told him to stop, he said that all the guys in the order room joked liked this and she was just being a prude.

He did stop calling her at work, however, but then began to call her at home. When she complained to the boss he said he couldn't do anything about it because the order clerk was on his own time: "That's just the way these guys are," he told Wanda. Is this sexual harassment?

Ellen was the only female student in her college physics class. When the professor lectured on the properties of concave and convex surfaces he informed the class that Ellen's chest was a good example of convex. The class laughed. He told them that now they would never forget the concept. Is this sexual harassment?

Debbie, who was a secretary, and her boss Greg were involved in a love affair. It had been a mutual attraction. After Debbie met Ralph she told Greg it was over between them. When her next performance review came up Greg rated Debbie as "Needing Improvement" and she did not get a raise. Is this sexual harassment?

If you said all these situations could be classified as sexual harassment you were right. These issues are highly charged. Frustrated supervisors and subordinates ask: "What did he mean by that?", "What does she want from me?", "If I ask him/her to lunch will he/she take it the wrong way?", "What happened to a sense of humor at work?"

Strategies

How does one survive, let alone get one's work done in a volatile atmosphere? We asked a few workplace survivors to talk about their own experiences.

Charna Norwood, a marine insurance underwriter, says that comments on a woman's appearance are not appropriate in the workplace for any reason. "When someone comments on my appearance I tell them to cut it out. I would tell working women, 'never laugh at a crude remark—don't let anyone have a good time at your expense.' Today, people are well aware when they're dancing on the edge."

Corporate attorney Gina Banks says, "Women can expect to be flirted with, innuendos will be made, and sometimes you will get out-and-out propositioned. I just act like it's not happening. I try not to do anything that would cause anyone to lose face. We have to work together and need to move on. I don't get caught up in it. You have to be careful because in my experience it will happen.

"You cannot send out wrong signals. You have to be aware and draw the boundaries. If you are in a situation where things are sliding toward trouble, you have to indicate that this is the end, or stop the behavior without being personally insulting."

Real estate broker Katherine Harris says, "I was in negotiations with a client for six months. Over the course of that time he would come to town and always bring me presents. He would give me candy. I would say 'thank you' and put it on my desk and immediately start discussing whatever business we had. I didn't give it any more attention than the 'thank you very much.'

"It became clear to him that the candy was just going to bring a thank you—nothing else. Men want to be in control, but they are easily embarrassed and easily threatened. You have to be clear without humiliating them."

Journalist Michael Sampson says that he's seen the workplace change dramatically. "Once I heard openly degrading comments about women on a regular basis in the newsroom. This happens much less frequently now. I've had to counsel some of my male staff members after I got complaints about their behavior. I've told them that the laws are very precise around this kind of thing."

Men's Confusion

But sometimes men just don't understand. They say they are confused because they thought they felt a mutual chemistry. They don't consider what they've done to be offensive. They don't see how women are being harmed. In fact, they feel that they were harmed by the complaint and they become angry.

Airline stewardess Tracey Mills says that she has learned a lot about the way men and women interact with each other in the course of her twelve years in the air.

"Men used to come on to me, make sexist jokes, and even touch me in ways I could swear I never encouraged. It enraged me until one day I had a conversation with a sociologist who was flying to San Francisco for a convention. He told me that he believed a lot of the confusion about appropriateness between men and women stems from our different interpretations of body language.

"'For example,' he said, 'when women listen to each other, or to men, they maintain eye contact for long periods of time, they tilt their heads as if they are hanging on every word, and from time to time they smile.

"'I used to think that all the women I knew believed I was fascinating and brilliant until I figured out this is the way the majority of women listen.

"'Then I realized that just because women nod and smile it doesn't mean they are agreeing with what I'm saying. Sometimes it only means they've heard it. It took me a long time and many, many misunderstandings to get this,' he said. 'Some men never do.'

"That man really helped me a lot," says Tracey. "I began to be more aware of my body language when I felt I was dealing with a potentially problematic customer."

A 1991 *New York Times*/CBS News Poll reported that 50 percent of male respondents admitted doing or saying something at work that could have been perceived as harassment. Forty percent of the females interviewed said they had experienced "sexual advances, propositions, and unwanted sexual discussions" from male supervisors or colleagues. Despite this high incidence, less than 10 percent of these women complained about the incidents.

Why did so few women complain? Some women fear they won't be believed, some fear for their jobs, others fear that complaining will only make the situation worse.

Geraldine Howe is a police officer in New York City. She says she knows other female officers who say they were harassed. "Some just didn't say anything about it," she says. "They wanted to stay on the job. Some waited a few years before they complained–until they could get safely transferred to other precincts. And these were pretty tough women. Others became radicalized and filed lawsuits. For them, the working relationship with the department was destroyed. Even if they won, they lost."

"A sexual harassment charge is probably the hardest thing in the world to prove," says labor attorney Andrea Marcus. "I won't say it's impossible, but it's very, very difficult. You need endless energy, stamina, and a very strong sense of yourself to go through depositions and eventually a jury trial to present your case. Believe me, a good defense attorney can make Mother Teresa look like a slut.

"I know this sounds terrible, but on the basis of my experience I'd counsel women to consider transferring or leaving a job rather than filing a charge."

But what if you can't leave? What if you can't go but you can't live with it, or you are so outraged that you feel you must do something?

Stopping Sexual Harassment

You can try to stop harassment in a variety of ways. Sometimes you unwittingly permit abuse by hesitating to cause a scene. Often you can stop sexual harassment simply by causing a scene.

You can tell the harasser to stop and threaten to tell everyone if he doesn't stop. If he continues, then you can make your threat good by telling everyone–*everyone.*

You can make sure you are never alone with the harasser by refusing to go into his office unless you bring someone with you, and by refusing to allow him into your office unless someone else is present. Even if you have to call your secretary or a colleague into your office ten times a day just because the harasser comes in, do it. People will begin to wonder what's going on and that should make him very nervous.

If this is not possible, then record your conversations with him. This can be done very unobtrusively in your office or in his. Carry a briefcase or a large folder with you with the portable recorder inside and ready to go. When you have finished, send him a copy of the tape.

Even if he catches you taping the conversation, this move can be very effective. You will have made your point and hopefully sent your harasser into a panic. In any event, he'll get the message that you mean business.

Filing a Charge

If none of these attempts proves successful and you decide that you want to file a formal charge against the harasser, the place to begin is your human resources or personnel department.

Your organization should have a separate procedure to deal with sexual harassment complaints that is different from its standard grievance procedure. This means you won't have to start the procedure with your boss–especially if your boss is the problem. The investigation will begin in the human resources department.

If the organization does not have a procedure set up that is different from the standard grievance procedure, then you need to go right to the top–or at least as high as you can in order to be heard. It is dangerous for a complaint like this to get buried in a bureaucratic grievance investigation. By law, once you make this kind of complaint known to management, they are under a strict obligation to investigate it. If they ignore it, they are liable, organizationally and personally, for damages.

What is a sexual harassment investigation like?

If conducted professionally, the investigation is a good faith attempt by a representative of the organization to determine what happened. The investigator will probe to see if there is a basis for the charge.

Some questions might include: Was the behavior of the accused harasser unwelcome? Was he told so? Was there a previous relationship between the individuals? Is corroboration available? Was anyone else told?

These are tough questions. To prepare for them it is a good idea to do some background work before filing a formal complaint. For example, while the harassment is going on someone should be told—preferably more than one person. A colleague or a friend—someone who will be able to substantiate the complaint once it has been made.

Also, it is important to confront the harasser and make it clear that his behavior is upsetting and/or offensive. At this point it would be advisable to ask colleagues for help. Then all conversations should be written up for the record and a copy sent to the personnel department. The complainer should request that a copy of this memo be time dated and kept in her own file for a period of one year.

Finally, it is helpful to keep a calendar or detailed log to note the dates and times the objectionable incidents took place. This will be invaluable to the investigator. The harasser will have to answer specific questions about those dates and times to the investigator's satisfaction.

Because you are dealing with varying levels of competence in an organization when it comes to conducting a sexual harassment investigation; because it is an uncomfortable assignment; and because in any organization there will continue to be "untouchables" (as long as we permit it) it is a good idea to be up front about the fact that you intend to file a charge with the Equal Employment Opportunity Commission if the harassment is not stopped.

Remember Moira in Chapter 1? Moira, if asked, probably would have said that sexual harassment was not her problem. Moira was bright, competent, and confident of her ability. While she was convinced the affair with her boss had nothing to do with her success, the staff assumed she was successful and powerful only because of the affair.

"An office affair is the kiss of death no matter who you are," says Jennifer Grady, a systems analyst. "Once you hop into bed with a boss or a colleague you play Russian roulette. You are fooling yourself if you think otherwise. Affairs confuse everyone. And everyone always finds out about them. And sadly it's still the woman who suffers."

Moira was able to start again, to be successful at another organization. But what effort it took–and two years of time. Her former boss, on the other hand, lost none of his power or prestige. She can no longer even think of him fondly. The affair, begun with such joy, and with assurances on both sides that it could be kept separate and distinct from the job, set Moira back in both her personal and professional life.

Sexual harassment hurts. It destroys spirits and ruins careers. When a woman experiences this behavior she should address it in some way. "Ignoring it is not the solution," says Andrea. "Yet, if you can't get justice, if you work for an organization that doesn't respect and support women, if you fear retaliation, then maybe the best response is to move on."

Sex will always be a factor in the workplace, but sexism needn't be. We probably can never expect to arrive at a time when the workplace will be sexually neutral. That's probably not even desirable, but we can expect our daughters to inherit a workplace where sexism has been eradicated. Sexism will become increasingly expensive to organizations, and those responsible for the financial drain will be replaced.

We never want to move to a place in this society where men become so intimidated they use the fear of being charged with sexual harassment as an excuse to stay away from women and to exclude them even more effectively from the circles of power.

Exclusion is deadly to any career because it limits exposure to the very people who can guide, support, and promote us. Nobody can do it all alone. Separate, as the Supreme Court has ruled, is not and never has been equal.

In Conclusion

The obstacles women face in their struggles for parity of pay and opportunity in the workplace are many and difficult.

Organizational politics, isolation, glass ceilings, cultural assumptions about women's capabilities to perform in certain capacities, organizational indifference to women's responsibilities as family caretakers, and sexual harassment–these are energy drainers and distracters that can impact performance and dampen enthusiasm.

When the male ego feels threatened, it attacks. Women experience the institutionalization of these attacks in the workplace when behaviors like teasing, threats, harassment, manipulation, and exclusion are permitted to flourish without penalty in an organization.

These behaviors allow those already in power to remain in power, and prevent those without power from acquiring it.

With competence, obstacles can be negotiated successfully and confronted effectively. So many women have repeatedly told us that competence is their most potent weapon in the struggle for visibility and parity.

Linda Michaelman is an attorney who counsels international corporate executives on the acquisition of companies. "They are concerned about the bottom line," she says. "They don't care if they deal with a man, a woman, or a goat as long as they get the quality of service they demand. But you *must* know what you are doing.

"It is very risky for a woman to be unprepared. A man will be given the benefit of the doubt, but when a woman makes a mistake it's often reduced to irrationality or emotionality."

Jane Fairmont, a restaurant supply sales manager agrees. "That's so important," she says. "There is no forgiveness. You have to be accurate and know what you are talking about every time you open your mouth. When you can do that they have no alternative but to respect you. They may not like you, or like working with you, but they have no basis on which to criticize you."

5

Making Your Ego Work for You

> *"I don't mind living in a man's world as long as I can be a woman in it."*
>
> *Marilyn Monroe*

*H*elene Falk is a successful Assistant District Attorney for the County of Los Angeles. She has tried and won cases that others have walked away from. Helene has a reputation for being tough. "It took me a long time to get where I am," she says. "I was a kid from the Bronx who always wanted something better. Now I have it. Believe me, there is no feeling in the world like winning a case. It is something that's so totally and completely yours. For me, it's still the ultimate thrill.

"The kick is when I went back East last Christmas my mother told me that although she was glad I was happy and proud that I was successful, she would never consider me 'settled' until I became a wife and mother.

"How do you think that makes me feel?" asks Helene sadly.

If female socialization was purposely designed to make our lives difficult, it would be hard to imagine any detail that was left out. Are there any benefits that come with female socialization?

Megan Smallwood, an executive search consultant, thinks so. She believes that women, because of the way we are socialized, have a natural inclination toward transformational management. "The *transformational* manager," she says, "is the leader who inspires and motivates his or her staff. This is in direct contrast to the *transactional* manager who tends to be over controlling and uses intimidation to meet deadlines."

Transformational Leadership

Remember Gail's boss, the telephone thrower, in Chapter 1? He was a transactional manager. He knew what needed to be done, he had the support of his manager, yet his style got in the way of his success. The staff, whose expertise was essential to getting the job done, literally walked out on him. The chief operating officer who protected him ultimately did the clinic a disservice.

"It's logical that we are natural leaders," Megan says. "We were brought up to be inclusive, to involve others in our problem solving, and always to be sensitive to how people are reacting to our behavior, our decisions, our talents, whatever.

"Now, I'm not saying that all women are transformational leaders," she adds. "While I have met some wonderful, inspiring women I have also met my share of barracudas. My point is that women already understand this way of interacting with people. They don't have to learn anything new to motivate them and engage them in the goals of the organization. They just have to remember."

Jenny Colon, Megan's partner, adds, "I believe the glass ceiling is a real factor in limiting transformational leaders to the middle management level. Some critics have said that transformational management works only in middle management and would never succeed at the top. I don't believe that. Transformational management is not generally practiced in top management because women are not generally there.

"If you look at the great managers who have moved companies forward, they have all practiced transformational leadership. I'm talking about men. The best of the best have operated this way. Ray Kroc of McDonald's, Sam Walton of Wal Mart, and Thomas J. Watson of IBM who said, 'We have respect for the individual.'"

In their 1982 best-seller, *In Search of Excellence*, Tom Peters and Robert Waterman observed that "Many of the best companies really do view themselves as an extended family. We found prevalent use of the specific terms 'family,' 'extended family,' or 'family feeling' at Wal Mart, Tandem, HP, Disney, Dana, Tupperware, McDonald's, Delta, IBM, Levi Strauss, Blue Bell, Kodak, and P & G." This positive impact will be increased when more women–more of the *right* women– become CEOs.

Empathy and Intuition

Yvette Coleman, a partner in a graphics firm says, "I've been told that I'm a good manager because I'm able to empathize with others. I understand the holistic quality of a person's life. A job is only one part of one's existence. We can celebrate the other important things in a person's life and still get the work done. We can take time to recognize them for a job well done. We get the payoff, really, in terms of the willingness of those people we treat decently to work hard and to have a positive outlook."

Some women claim to have more finely developed intuitive skills than men, although there is some controversy about this among both men and women.

"Women do have strong intuition," says Vera Keath, a finance manager, "and it is a result of our socialization. But making a good decision also requires rigorous analytic skills. A large part of my business is judgment. I can't say that intuition gives me an edge."

Remember Jeanette and Dave in Chapter 1? Jeanette might disagree. She says she knew something was "not right" during her first interview with Dave. Despite the fact that based on skills, education, and experience he appeared to be the logical choice for the job, she knew something was wrong.

Jeanette overrode her intuition however. She believed her

"feelings" were a handicap in dealing logically and decisively with situations now that she was part of management. She lived to regret the day she ignored that internal alarm.

Because the workplace is a world where logic, reason, and consistency are valued, women tend to be ambivalent about owning "left brain" skills.

Clifford Joiner, a career naval officer, says that he doesn't believe there is any unique intuition that only women possess. "I don't think women are any more intuitive than men," he says. "What I do believe is that everyone knows when something feels right and when it just doesn't. This goes for starting a new job or for buying a home. First impressions shouldn't be ignored.

"But, some of us are better at ignoring intuition than others." Cliff says, "Because men are more prone to ignoring it, we value it in the men who don't ignore it. We seek out other men whose 'hunches' and 'impressions of a guy' we trust when we have to make a decision."

Values

"I believe," says Joyce Williams, a physician's assistant, "that women approach their work in a value-driven way. Men are more willing to close their eyes to problems. When women point out the problems they say we are "difficult." It's just that men don't think details are important. And they accuse us of being obsessed with details.

"At my last job nurse aides were working out of title. They were assigned some tasks the nurses should have been doing. Well, I made a big noise about it. I was 'difficult.' It was a matter of patient safety. How would you like someone who wasn't trained properly working on you or on a member of your family?

"Men think someone else will take care of the details—will clean up after them. For doctors it has traditionally been the nurses. Men think that detail is only important when it catches up with them. Remember the Senate banking scandal? Nobody thought about detail. Nobody thought it was important until everybody got caught! I know I sound rigid, but that would never have happened to a group of women!"

Sensitivity

Little girls are encouraged to be aware of others' feelings, to make others comfortable, and to include them in activities and conversation. As a result, by the time most women reach adulthood, they have developed an eye for nonverbal cues and signals in the body language of others. This ability is developed so slowly over time that many women are not even conscious of it. They operate on the basis that everyone sees what they see.

Joan, a systems analyst, remembers the time her boss was discussing a new procedure he wanted her and three other programmers to implement. He specified a three-month time frame. She watched as one of the programmers listened in a nervous and distracted way. He repeatedly assured the boss there was no problem with the deadline.

Joan noticed the programmer's head moved slowly from side to side as he spoke. "I knew he would be useless on the project," she says. "I could see he had no intention of cooperating. It just wasn't a priority for him. And he was useless. And the boss never saw it coming."

Putting Others First

Ava Gough, a sales executive for an operating room equipment supply company, says when she has problems on the job it is sometimes easy for her to overlook the positive aspects of the way she was socialized. "The down side of being raised to put others first and to take a supportive role is more apparent to me at those times, and I resent it," she says.

"For example, I was raised to be either a nurse or a teacher. Those were the top careers for women when I was growing up. Well, I became the nurse, and my sister became the teacher. Our younger brother went to medical school. The message was clear back then, and we never thought there was anything wrong with it. Women were assigned 'light duty' while they waited for Prince Charming to rescue them."

Ava says she was angry for many years. In her own life Prince Charming just passed through, and she is now a single mother supporting a teenage son and eight-year-old twins. "I went back to school," she says. "I took a risk by going into sales and nobody was more surprised than I when I became successful. My attitude started changing after that.

"I run a division now and my staff is the most productive team in the company. We always come in above goal–and we enjoy working together. Some of the success is due, I really believe, to 'placing others first and taking a supportive role.' It kills me to admit it. I call it other things, of course, like 'respect for and nurturance of the staff.'"

Ava sees a distinct difference between the way she approaches sales management and the approaches her male colleagues use.

"I believe it's a matter of focus. Today I'm glad I was encouraged to focus outwardly. Focusing inwardly, trying to grab all the credit and toss all the blame, seems very exhausting to me.

"One of the other sales managers is always telling me what he's done for his staff. Most of the women managers I know tell me how much their staff has contributed to the company. It's just a different point of reference.

"Anyway, this colleague of mine was overheard talking to one of the vice presidents about a sales rep on his staff. He said, 'I gave that kid $75,000 last year.' It got back to her and she was livid. She went right into his office and said to him, 'You didn't give me anything. I earned over $100,000 last year and you paid me $75,000.'

"He had no idea why she was so angry. You see, his socialization was very different from ours. He was brought up to be the provider, the protector, the source of power, and the most important person in his orbit. He really felt betrayed. 'After all I did for her . . . .' he said to me."

A Sense of Timing

The "outward focus" Ava talks about also provides some women with an advantage when it comes to timing. Good timing is knowing when to intervene before problems become crises. It's knowing when to speak with a person, when to wait, and when to cut your losses.

"Good timing means being able to 'read' others," says newscaster Ramona Whitt, "especially the person at the top. You have to study the conditions that are most favorable for you to approach the boss to get what you need and learn under what conditions you don't have a prayer—even if your proposal is brilliant.

"This takes patience, and women have that, God knows. You can lose opportunities by being too enthusiastic and presenting your idea at the wrong time. Someone else will pick up that idea and run with it at the right time if you're not careful.

"If you have the type of boss who usually supports the last proposal he hears, then get out of the way. Let the others make their presentations and just make sure that yours is the last human voice he hears on the subject."

Martha Wolf, an art buyer, remembers that as a little girl growing up in a house with two brothers and three sisters it was the girls who were not permitted to fight. "My brothers," she says, "were allowed to settle their differences in any way they chose—up to and including bashing each other. The girls were punished for raising their voices.

"At the time I thought all this was terribly unfair. When we were at a safe distance from our parents, my sisters and I would sometimes resort to resolution by a good slap, but it didn't happen often. Someone would always snitch. It was very frustrating, let me tell you.

"Today, however, I look at it a little differently. In order to survive in that household the females had to learn to compromise and negotiate. We had to handle conflict, competition, and misunderstandings in creative and what my mother called 'civilized' ways.

"Today I'm glad I learned to do that. In my job I've found that knowing how to resolve disagreements among staff members and preserve relationships pays off."

Lessons from the Martial Arts

The skills of listening, identifying options, negotiating solutions, and setting a future course where everybody wins something and saves some face goes a long way to maintaining productivity and reducing turnover rates. If these are "soft skills" it is very interesting that corporations are spending so many dollars training their managers to be able to accomplish just these things.

Our economic rivals, the Japanese, have appreciated these skills for centuries. They believe that some of the most important abilities an executive can have are intuitive–especially precise timing and an appreciation for indirection and "face saving."

The Japanese acknowledge the interdependency of people in the workplace and the necessity for "WA" or group harmony. Hero and Star status are discouraged. Loyalty to one's group is one of the most respected attributes of Japanese managers. Sensitivity and nurturing skills–"women's concerns" in the West–are business concerns in the East.

Richard Pascale and Anthony Athos, in their 1981 bestseller, *The Art of Japanese Management* observe that team experiments in the United States often fail because American managers don't realize what they are creating requires a lot of energy and attention to sustain.

When American managers complain that subordinates are too dependent, want too much attention, expect too much of them, or want to be "coddled" they are really saying they are uncomfortable and embarrassed at having to do what has traditionally been assigned to women in our culture. Nurturance is for mothers, not fathers!

Warren Morton, a corporate attorney, observes that it is curious that the Japanese have become our main competition in the world economy. "Their samurai mentality is so very different from our American cowboy mentality," he says. "Strong Japanese males like flowers and poetry. They appreciate things that the American male associates with femininity and weakness.

"The Japanese corporate samurai mentality is not afraid to fail," Warren says. "When they do fail they look at it not as a sign of weakness, but as a situation they can learn from and they move ahead. They are not afraid of retreat but see it as simply taking a step back–a successful long-term strategy.

"Women," he says, "are more like the Japanese samurai. They bring a broader perspective to the work environment. They have the ability to be more responsive and to listen. Women are just as capable of moving an organization forward as men–they just do it in a different way. I urge women not to abandon the values that make them different from men. I think femininity is not antithetical to business management. It is an added dimension that is a positive force in propelling an organization forward."

Control

The Japanese have become extraordinarily successful in business in part by paying attention to some of the things that American businessmen have discounted. For example, as Pascale and Athos observe, the Japanese accept ambiguity, uncertainty, and imperfection as givens in organizational life. They know that the appearance of control is sometimes an illusion.

Control is difficult for American managers to give up. Male managers find it especially hard to let go because in the workplace control is tangible proof that one has power. Jeremy Wonder, a commodities trader, observes that, "Power in industry has always been defined as controlling the behavior of subordinates and yes, of colleagues too, despite their opposition. The more opposition you overcome, the more power you have."

In addition, American men have been trained to take a very rigid approach to problem solving. Facts and statistics are extremely important to them. The process of moving from start to finish is also critical. There is one accepted path clearly understood by other men. This is the path of "logical sequence." Too much speculation of "looseness" in the planning process makes them nervous–it feels too much like chaos.

Joe Tannenbaum in his book, *Male and Female Realities*, cites an excellent example of this difference. He calls it women's "holistic" and men's "linear" approach:

> A woman gives a solution to a problem five minutes after the meeting begins. Her solution is accurate, but the men can't hear it because they're not ready for it. They haven't been through the "a, b, c, d" steps yet. The men will talk and argue; then an hour later, a man will give the exact same solution as the woman's. All the men will say, "Yes that's dead on; that's what we should do." The woman has no alternative but to think that men simply don't listen to her because she is a woman. The fact is, the men didn't listen to her not because the information was being offered by a woman, but because they were not ready for the information. If a man had made the same suggestion out of sequence, it would also have been ignored.

The Japanese manager takes a more philosophical approach to change, control, and progress. He experiences existence in more fluid terms–terms that Western women understand, but which make Western men feel very uncomfortable.

Much of this orientation is a result of the cultural influence of Zen Buddhism. Zen places a higher value on the intuition over the intellect. Enlightenment in the Zen philosophy is achieved by attaining freedom from passion and illusion. Indeed, Zen considers individuality an illusion. Clearly, this is why the notion of "corporate heroes" and "superstars" is so foreign to the Japanese businessman.

Order is maintained through balance, or harmony between opposing forces. Undesirable imbalance occurs when one force becomes prominent or dominant.

Nurturance

Japanese organizations are geared to the long haul, not only in the transaction of business, but in the development and nurturance of the staff. The assumption is that we will be working or doing business together for a long time. Differences must be settled, decisions must be made, but relationships should be retained in the process. Compare this with what Warren has called the American cowboy mentality where direct action, decisiveness, objectivity, and having "the guts to fire someone" are valued as key managerial attributes. Rather than building on what we have we seem more anxious to wipe the slate clean and begin again.

Women are the relationship caretakers in our culture. They have the potential to activate these Eastern values in the American workforce because they understand them so well. They have grown up with them.

Eastern values emphasize accommodation, slow change, reliance on personal experience in decision making, and accepting the reality of dependence on others. The Japanese do not see the individual as the center of the universe. They accept certain levels of ambiguity and ambivalence in corporate life. They do not deny these realities but accommodate them by working problems through in staff teams.

Pascale and Athos note the "Japanese view of groups is most closely analogous to that toward marital relationships in the West—and interestingly the Japanese recognize the kinds of problems and concerns in work relationships that we focus on in marriage concerning trust, sharing and commitment."

One American manager did recognize it, and quite by accident. The corporate training division of Eugenics Industries had everything going for it. The staff was enthusiastic, creative, and extremely competent. The only problem was they couldn't work together. The trainers could not get along with each other and the organization development specialist could not get along with any of them. Petty jealousies, territoriality, and personality clashes were slowly destroying what should have been a successful division.

Valerie Nichols, director of this mess, was becoming disheartened. Valerie had hired each staff member herself. They were all her first choices. She had hired on the basis of competence and potential and had frankly not given sufficient thought to how this group of high-powered trainers would interact.

Valerie made some attempts at team building through planning sessions and brainstorming meetings, but nothing lasted over time. They would try to move their plans along, but somehow ego would get in the way. Someone was always hurt, someone was always angry. Everyone was frustrated. They all knew they were better than this.

Valerie tried to analyze the problems and one afternoon it struck her that the bickering, the lack of trust, the struggles over budget, and jealousies over the spotlight were issues that were very similar to those that had brought her and her husband to the brink of divorce a year ago.

Could it be so simple? Valerie wondered. She really didn't have much to lose, or for that matter any time to waste. Some of the trainers would have to be replaced if she could not get them to work together.

Valerie opened her phone book and dialed Hal Goodwin, her marriage counselor. She asked if he would consider a group project. One week later five trainers, an organization development specialist, and Valerie went into marital counseling.

Hal interviewed each separately and then took the group offsite for a full day. Based on the interviews and with the knowledge that competence was not an issue for this group, Hal concentrated on three areas–style differences, communication skills, and conflict resolution. He told them they were going to spend the day removing the combat from their conversation and learning how to listen to each other.

First he administered a personality styles test to each staff member and released the results to the group. The trainers began to understand how their personality "types" interacted with the personality "types" of their co-workers. They saw how their bent toward extraversion or introversion affected their perceptions, attitudes, and judgments. They began to understand why and how they acted the way they did and why their behavior might be a problem for the others.

Don preferred to get things settled before he moved on to something else. Diane preferred to keep options open. He was a "judging" type and she a "perceptive" type. Janet, an extravert, liked variety and action and often was impatient when an assignment dragged on. Jean, on the other hand, was an introvert who liked to concentrate on one thing at a time and despised intrusion and interruption.

Jody, a "feeling" type, liked to please people, was sympathetic toward others, and looked for an occasional pat on the back from Valerie. Dave, on the other hand, was often blunt. He was an "analytical" type who showed little emotion himself and was very uncomfortable dealing with other people's feelings.

The test confirmed what they had suspected. Each saw the world in a very different way and assumed the others were deliberately acting with the intention of making their lives miserable.

Everybody's approach to people and to problems was different. That was clear. It was no longer reasonable to attribute the others' irritating behavior to spitefulness or deceit. Jody began to understand why she could not expect a warm collegial relationship with Dave, and Jean and Janet made a pact never to even consider sharing an office again. It was too frustrating to try to accommodate each other.

So, instead of focusing on the friction, they began to divide the workload by personality type strengths. Through role playing and short exercises Hal helped the group determine how they were going to communicate in the future. They developed models for conflict resolution by setting ground rules for acceptable behavior and outlawing dirty fighting when differences arose.

Finally, they prepared an action plan. This solidified their determination to work together to build a successful division. Everyone had a role, everyone took an active part, and there were rules and guidelines set up to handle the struggles they all knew would come. All were enthusiastic and determined to give this a shot, based on their new insights into themselves and into each other.

Hal followed up with them twice during the year. "We wouldn't exactly call it a miracle," says Valerie, "but there was an extraordinary change. They had learned to work together effectively and became more productive than any of them had imagined they could be."

Applying the very teachable "soft" skills of active listening, consensus building, and conflict resolution, the atmosphere changed and the productivity that had been trapped by the serious human relations problems was released. A real business solution to a real business problem . . . Eastern style . . . Female style.

In Conclusion

In focusing on coping with the male ego in the workplace we must be careful not to lose sight of the considerable strengths of the female ego.

Socialized to support, defer, and maintain the peace, we are finding that the very qualities that cause us so much anxiety also can be used to great advantage in the workplace.

As society's designated, relationship caretakers we understand the importance of trust, sharing, and commitment. Organizations are recognizing the importance of these values in motivating and developing staff, and are sending their male executives to seminars and institutes to learn to incorporate them into their management styles.

Women, raised with these values, bring to organizations the skills of negotiation, patience, supportiveness, empathy, inclusiveness, and the ability to compromise. Through the use of social skills to resolve interpersonal conflict, women have shown an extraordinary ability to resolve disagreements while preserving relationships. We also appear to be more able to tolerate and promote collaborative management styles and systems of shared power.

Japanese managers have demonstrated the business value of these strengths and have clearly gotten the attention of

American managers. The challenge to American women is to refuse to permit our skills to be valued while our gender continues to be devalued. Men who develop female skills should not become more valued by an organization than the women who already have them.

6

Making His Ego Work for You

"I have found some of the best reasons I ever had for remaining at the bottom simply by looking at the men at the top."

F.M. Colby

*T*he staff meeting was over. Four designers clustered together in the hall rehashing the last hour.

"What does he want from us?" Joanne sighed.

"I don't think he knows himself," growled Howard.

"Well, I know what it's all about," said Jackie smugly. "He'd love to get us going at each other. Did you see the way he tried to get Doug to believe Joanne had set up the whole fall shirt line without talking to him?"

"Indeed I did," Joanne said. "He just wants to keep the heat off himself–he doesn't want us banding together against him."

"Well, it's a good thing I know better, Jo," said Doug. "But I'll tell you what–he's going to have to beg me for my sketches for the client meeting. I'm not giving him a thing until he asks for it."

"Nothing pleases him anyway," Jackie added. "Why doesn't he give it up? We're all on to him. None of his nonsense works on us anymore." They all laughed.

He Is the Boss

The boss. That most maligned of individuals. Creator of worker's misery, maker of stupid decisions, promoter of low pay. The Great Chief who's second guessed, gossiped about, ridiculed and whose downfall is ardently prayed for. Jane Fonda concluded, "You can run an office without a boss, but you can't run an office without secretaries." She even made a movie about it.

Who would want such a job?

Men. Men like being the boss. Being "in charge" excites most men. It's where they eventually expect to be if they are not there already. Men don't wonder about whether or not they are suited to be the boss. They rarely agonize about power. They don't take assertiveness training and "coping with difficult subordinates" courses to get them ready.

Men are already ready. They have been raised to feel special and able to lead. They have ample role models around them to give them confidence and something concrete to aspire to.

In America most organizations are hierarchical and most of the power at the top rests in the hands of men. Some men exercise their power reasonably and fairly–and then there are the manipulators and the exploiters, like Joanne's boss.

A bad boss can spell career disaster for an ambitious woman. Bosses should be chosen very carefully. Like high-price items and important relationships, the fit must be right or no one is comfortable. Failed boss-subordinate relationships always result in anger. Recovery from a bad work situation can take a long time.

How does a woman choose the right boss? Women who shared their experiences with us suggest it is helpful to identify the kinds of support we need from a boss. We must clarify, in our own minds, what kind of support we are looking for and use our needs as criteria when we interview with a boss for a job or for a promotion.

Women who expect to be coached should look for a boss who is clearly willing to mentor. Women in other circumstances, like re-entering the workforce after a long period of caretaking, might require simply direction and a paycheck. Their criteria might include fairness, clarity, and evenness of temper.

Clara Meeves worked for the same company for thirty years. She says she always made sure she understood what the boss wanted. "I obeyed the rules," she said, "and taught myself never to get entangled in any dispute with a male supervisor.

"I believed it was better to maintain a low profile because they could get upset about things other than the work, and heads would roll. I would be reminded of my daughter's tuition and our mortgage payment and when something happened that I found offensive, like stealing my ideas or dumping extra work on me, I bit my tongue and bore the insult."

Not all women are as long suffering as Clara, but so many who spoke with us are very frustrated. They are coping with offensive and disrespectful behavior from their bosses that they find difficult to confront.

Take the case of Nora Harrison who says, "I wish I could be more candid. I spend time trying to figure out how to present something to my boss so that it will be heard. If I am too clear or act insistent, my boss accuses me of being strident. He will argue with my male colleagues when they take a hard line but me he tries to diminish . . . ."

Karen Price once had a boss who publicly admitted his low opinion of women. He even went so far as to tell her it was not his idea to work with her–it was something he had been told he had to do. He believed women were not capable of handling complex jobs.

"We were forced to work together on a series of projects." Karen says, "I found out by his responses, certainly not by his manners, that he came to respect my opinions. In meetings we would discuss an issue. He would lay out his demands. When I disagreed I never said so directly. Instead, I would say 'have you thought about this factor, or that variable,' something like that.

"I would explain what I meant briefly, support it with key points, and then let it go. I did not argue with him. He would interrupt, be abrupt, sometimes abrasive, however, he would listen and ask an occasional question. Afterwards, I never called him or said anymore about the subject. I just waited.

"He would come back a few days later, after having thought about the issue, or after having discussed it with his superiors. He would inform me of the next steps. It became clear he was using 60 percent of my suggestions and recommendations. He would present my approach as his own. Can you imagine? It was predictable, of course.

"Instead of being furious, I felt triumphant and complimented. I chose to respond this way. It was important to me to demonstrate that women had something important to contribute. Gradually, he behaved more respectfully towards me and towards other professional women in the firm."

Coping with difficult interpersonal issues between male bosses and female subordinates can be so draining that productivity suffers. How do we handle ourselves effectively when the male ego overtakes the male boss? How can we change the equation?

Let's look at three types of bosses as prime examples of the male ego in action. The male ego is a manifestation of a strong need to control. This behavior compensates for a basic feeling of insecurity.

The Male Ego, as we use the term, describes the behavior of those who expend a large portion of their energy maintaining a sense of superiority by keeping others in an inferior or disadvantaged position. It is recognizable in the language these men speak, in their body language, and in their inability to hide their discomfort with women.

These classic types—which we have structured as composite characters in order to focus our observations are "The Hoarder," "The Hysteric," and "The Controller." The behavior they display can make working life hell for women. Women must learn how to interact effectively with them in order to succeed and to maintain their own sense of integrity.

The Hoarder

Let's call him Arnie, of the *genus* "Anal Retentive." For Arnie information is power. When you work for Arnie he excludes you from meetings because he must be the sole conduit of information. (Of course, you receive only about half of the information that you need from him.)

Arnie does not appreciate your meeting with other colleagues–either at your level or at his–for any reason. He worries about what you are going to say. Be forewarned–Arnie is extremely defensive if you call him on any of his behavior. He will swear that he gives you all the information that is appropriate for you to have.

When you request anything of Arnie–a day off, a new chair, yesterday's sales figures, Arnie stalls. He can't help himself. Arnie likes to keep his options open. He will tell you he never makes spur of the moment decisions–how true! The problem is you never get a response. Arnie hopes you will forget, or you will get tired of asking.

Donna Hooper knows Arnie well. "I have had to learn to manage my boss," she says. "That's a more difficult challenge than the job I'm paid to do. I have actually had to work his ego in order to prevent his ego from working or controlling me. It takes a lot of flexibility and a lot of compromise.

"When I was learning this job I would ask my boss how to do something and he'd say 'don't be so curious.' Finally I figured out that if I treated him like an authority I'd get the information I needed. It was when I began to ask his opinion about issues and asked how he might handle each of the tasks I was assigned that I began to get the information I needed. As long as I did things his way he stopped encouraging the other men to undermine me.

"It was such a simple thing, really. So simple I almost missed it. I grew up in a single-parent home with four sisters. I'm used to dealing and struggling with women, but let me tell you it's very different from struggling with the male ego.

"I began to send him memos documenting everything I did. I realized how much he loved paper. I created agendas and requested meetings with him. I always let him know where I would be, and when I needed to deal with one of the other departments I always asked if he wanted to attend the meeting. I suggested that if he authorized me to handle it for him it would take some of the burden off him. Sometimes he agreed, sometimes he refused. I began every memo with 'If you have no objection . . . .'

"The process was exhausting in the beginning. It was like trying to win over a wary child. He really believed women were incapable of handling senior-level positions in our firm and was fully prepared to let the men who reported to him finish me off professionally. Once I convinced him I wasn't a threat and that my competence could make him look good he relaxed and called my colleagues off.

"We work together well now, but I still resent what I call my 'hazing' period. My male colleagues did not have to go through anything like that. Other women in this company gave up in rage or despair. I'm still here because I'm so determined and I was willing to stroke his ego until I was able to get what I needed to do my work.

"I would counsel other women to find out early how strong your boss's ego needs are, so that you don't exhaust yourself trying to swim upstream." Donna says, "Sometimes you have to be satisfied with playing a secondary role for a while, even when you know you are smarter and more capable than the person in charge. It hurts, but unfortunately if you want to succeed, sometimes it is a necessary first step for women."

The Hysteric

Let's call him Harry. For Harry everything is a priority and the priorities are always changing. Every issue carries the same weight. Everything is first on his list.

Harry is sure that anything that can, will go wrong. He translates this belief into a series of self-fulfilling prophecies. Everything around Harry usually does go wrong. He lives with disaster on a daily basis.

Harry makes impulsive decisions and is constantly second guessing everyone on his staff. He will have to stop and start a project so many times that you will begin to doubt yourself. What you produce for Harry is never quite what he asked you for–never. You are always "a shade off," or "one frame out of sync."

Evelyn Miller speaks from experience about her own Harry. "I am very careful about revealing mistakes, tentativeness, or weakness to my boss," she says. "He delights in catching subordinates–especially female subordinates–in some discrepancy. He uses coarse language with the men but tries to temper his expletives with the women. This is because he believes he is being respectful of women. Actually, it's because he thinks we don't belong in his department.

"My boss believes the work we do is so critical and so difficult that he is the only one capable of doing it right. If he could work twenty-four hours a day he would. If he could clone himself, he would. But he can't. The next best thing to cloning himself is to hire men who are as driven as he is. That's his preference.

"In his eyes the workplace is a man's world. He wants women to remain comforters, nurturers, mothers, and daughters. He finds it very difficult to deal with women who clearly don't fit any of those roles. He loves his mother and his daughter dearly, but his wife and his female subordinates are great sources of irritation to him because we have all forgotten our place.

"Harry is very uneasy about delegating work to women. If he must, he follows up so closely and is involved in so much detail that any sense of satisfaction we might get from a project is lost.

"Because he believes, despite all of this, that he really likes women he refuses to come down as hard publicly on us as he does on the men when something goes wrong. When a woman screws up, he admonishes her privately and tries to convince her that she'd be happier in another department. This makes it so difficult for us to work together as colleagues. It's not fair to the men, and there's no growth for the women.

"The last time I missed one of his impossible deadlines and he gave us a pep talk about being happier elsewhere I agreed with him," says Evelyn. "His face lit up and his hysteria actually seemed to subside. I had applied for a job at his level.

I knew it was a long shot, and I knew I couldn't count on him for support, but I had built alliances and gained supporters within the company.

"Well, I got the job and the day I told him was the sweetest day of my life. He was so shocked he couldn't contain how he felt. 'A woman can't do that job,' he said. 'It's too intense, you have to supervise too many men, there's so much travel involved . . . .'

"But a woman is going to," I said. "See you at the next senior staff meeting–I'll save you a seat."

Millie Vargas, an insurance claims adjuster, has another story to tell. "I had a boss who had to be right in an almost childlike way." She says, "If I did not agree with him, I was the one who was difficult. He actually threw tantrums, banged on the desk, and hollered when he was angry. His hysteria would break into rage at a moment's notice."

Millie was not as fortunate as Evelyn. She could not escape through promotion. Her firm was small and upward mobility was limited.

Millie had to figure out how to keep both her self-esteem and her paycheck. "It wasn't easy," she says.

"Sometimes his tantrums made me feel confused and frightened. I'd become tongue-tied and couldn't answer him and that made things worse. It was so humiliating that I began to avoid him whenever I could. I sent all my progress reports to him in writing. If there was a way to communicate with him that didn't involve being in the same room, I used it.

"I got all my work done, met all my deadlines, and satisfied my customers, but a strange thing began to happen. He seemed to forget all about me. He no longer accused me of being difficult, but he no longer demanded anything of me. It was like I wasn't there.

"The stress was gone, but I stopped getting challenging assignments and my presence was required at fewer and fewer meetings. I didn't know what to do, so I talked the situation over with my brother who is a former marine and now is lieutenant in the police department. I figured he must have dealt with some impossible men in his time.

"'Millie,' he said. 'You've got to get back into the arena. You've got to stand up for yourself in your dealings with him or you'll just fade into the background and pretty soon you'll be out of a job.'

"'You're acting like a victim,' he said. 'You're playing right into his image of you–probably his image of all women–as not tough enough and not able to keep up with him.'

"The very next morning I went into my boss's office and asked for the Anderson account, which I knew was a high-profile case. "I didn't have much hope of getting the assignment, but it gave me a reason to see him. He looked at me as if he had trouble remembering who I was.

"'What makes you think you're qualified to handle the Anderson case?' he asked.

"'I'm qualified because I'm a good adjuster,' I said, 'I've been on the job ten years, I'm thorough, I'm persistent, and I have good follow through.'

"'Jamesway has been assigned to the case,' he growled. 'He's aggressive and he's smart.'

"'How do you know how aggressive I can be unless you give me a chance?' I asked, my heart pounding loudly.

"'If you're so damned aggressive, where the hell have you been?' he thundered.

"At that point I stood up. 'I don't think you heard me,' I said as slowly as I could. 'I'm a good adjuster and I need more complicated assignments so that I can move ahead. I've been in the background lately and I want to change that.'

"Now he was interested. 'You'll have to take your turn in the rotation like everyone else,' he said, 'and you'll have to participate more in group meetings, and you'll have to deal more directly with me.'

"'We're both adults,' I said, with more confidence than I felt, 'and we should be able to deal with each other in a reasonable way.'

"'We'll see,' he mumbled.

"Our relationship remained difficult, but it was no longer overwhelming for me. I had established a basis for dialogue. When he became impossible, I was able to confront his behavior by suggesting we set aside another time to discuss the problem, a time when both of us could be more reasonable. I began refusing to get up from the chair in his office until he heard me out–no matter how abusive he got. I'd just wait until he finished, and then I'd begin. Finally, I started giving him credit publicly from time to time for the success I had.

"I learned that his behavior was pure bluster, childish rage. It was unpleasant, but not dangerous to me personally or professionally. If I had the strength to stand up to it as my brother had counseled me, I could work with it.

"My male colleagues tease that I get more from him because I'm a woman. I laugh along with them but I don't believe that's true at all. We hammered out a working relationship when I stopped being afraid of him and he stopped seeing me as fragile."

Alonda Daniels, an administrative assistant for a chemical processing firm, dealt with a screaming boss in a very different, but no less effective way.

"When he raised his voice," she says with a smile, "I lowered mine. When he screamed, I whispered. It threw him completely off balance. I always responded in the same way, and I always told him I couldn't do my work when he yelled at me.

" 'It's so disconcerting,' I said. 'Every time you yell it sets me back a full day.'

"Change didn't happen over night," Alonda says, "but change did happen. He deals with me in a respectful and reasonable way now, and I didn't have to exhaust myself fighting with him about it.

"I used the oldest of female stereotypes–'the lady'–to my great advantage. It worked. We have to be very resourceful when we deal with men in the workplace."

The Control Freak

Let's observe Buttoned-Up Burt, the Control Freak. Burt is the boss who appears to do everything right. He delegates, requests input from the staff, and prides himself on his open door policy. He is also the boss who never lets go of any real authority. Burt must be in control.

Burt likes to divide and conquer. Joanne's boss, who we met at the beginning of this chapter, is a classic Buttoned-Up Burt. He likes to keep his staff just a bit off balance. When they struggle with each other the focus comes off Burt and he can busy himself checking on their operations.

Burt rummages in the ranks of his organization. While he holds his managers responsible for their areas, he deals directly with their subordinates, countermands their orders, and revises their plans–all in the guise of being helpful. He is perhaps the most destructive boss an ambitious woman can have because he envisions himself mentoring his female subordinates while in actuality he is undermining them.

Ask Kay. Remember Kay from Chapter 1? She was the senior vice president who had to fire the boss's favorite. Kay's boss encouraged direct access to himself for Kay's employee, Sam. He gave Sam advice, direction, and even made interventions for him with Kay.

Burt so undermined Kay's authority that when she suspended Sam it seemed natural to him to appeal directly to Burt. Kay had confronted her Burt on several occasions about his propensity to manage her staff while holding her responsible for the results. She was given the classic "bear with me" defense and the explanation that "this is just the way I am."

Kay even tried to manage the problem through her subordinates by insisting they share with her any conversations or directions they received from her boss.

Still, her authority steadily eroded. The staff began to play to Burt, and Kay increasingly felt caught in the middle of a process that was being played out all around her. Burt tried to make light of his behavior, even though he knew it troubled Kay, by telling her in a self-deprecating way that she was a "workaholic," a "micro-manager," and a "stickler for detail." He tried to mitigate her anger by complimenting her for being able to "put up with him." It made Kay furious.

"In retrospect," Kay says, "I did the best I could with a bad situation. I kept it all out on the table. I confronted my boss each time he engaged Sam, and told him that his behavior not only made me uncomfortable but made it increasingly difficult for me to supervise Sam.

"I also put Sam on notice that he was to advise me each time the boss changed a directive I gave him or even talked about making changes. Sam knew he would have to deal with me if I heard it from someone else first.

"What I was really doing though," she says, "was reacting to everyone. If I was in the same situation today, I think I'd take a more pro-active approach. I'd request weekly meetings with Burt and bring Sam along. I'd insist that all issues concerning Sam's unit be discussed at those meetings.

"In this way I'd create a forum to work through issues with my boss in front of Sam. I think that would have salvaged some of my credibility as Sam's boss. I'd also be able to confront my boss in front of Sam if the terms of our agreement were broken. Nobody likes to be caught breaking his word. It would have given me some leverage.

"I think this would have given me the sense that I was still in control. I concentrated too much on damage control behind the scenes. If I had it to do again, I would insist that we all meet together at a regularly scheduled time and agree that no business was to be transacted outside those meetings.

"It would have saved a lot of wear and tear on me, and it could have kept me from feeling so angry with my boss all the time."

Your Anger

Difficult bosses invariably provoke anger in their subordinates. Anger is a natural emotion, but one that has destructive potential–especially for women. Often male colleagues dismiss an angry woman as irrational. She is described as bitchy, strident, shrill, and inappropriate.

Women must learn to use anger effectively in the workplace. We must force ourselves to deal with bosses or colleagues who anger us just as Millie, Alonda, Evelyn, and Kay did.

Being able to be directly angry at someone can communicate your respect for that person. It takes a lot of strain off a relationship and it communicates to others how important an issue is to you–especially if you don't get angry very often. Harriet Goldhor Lerner, in her work *The Dance of Anger*, says that it takes courage to know when we are angry and to let others hear about it. "When we [women] voice our anger ineffectively, however, without clarity, direction, and control it may in the end be assuring to others. We allow ourselves to be written off and provide others with an excuse for not taking us seriously."

Anger should never be allowed to fester. If it is possible to consistently assert yourself to a difficult boss, as Millie was able to do, you can avoid the build-up of resentments that can ultimately result in a blowup over something minor. If you allow your anger to balloon and blow it is a sure bet you will be labeled irrational and accused of overreacting to a minor incident.

"It's hard when you're a subordinate to deal with condescension or other prejudices of corporate life," says Jeanne Steele. "It's very hard to make a person understand unless it is egregious. As a black woman, there is all the usual behavior I deal with–being overtly passed over for a job, feeling invisible, coping with ingratiating behavior . . . . "

"That's so true," agrees Raya Santos. "It helps me when I look right at the person and say 'I don't understand what you meant by that remark.' I make my boss explain what he has said and I *never* smile as I ask him to clarify himself.

"When my boss considers people to promote to open positions or to serve on projects or task forces he doesn't even think of a minority person or a woman. That makes me very angry because it is so consistent."

"What makes *me* angry," says Judy Lennon, "is that women have the extra burden of having to balance their image. We seem to be required to present ourselves in the workplace as both feminine and competent. Men's competency is not at odds with their masculinity. It's just one more thing . . . . "

Women who discussed their anger with us advise other

women to delay their response to their boss if they are very angry. Listen to what is being said, they caution. Set up a second meeting if you feel too angry to cope with it at the time. It is acceptable to express anger in the workplace. A display of hysteria or tears, however, is unacceptable–either will kill your credibility. Delay your response; do not allow yourself to be perceived as not being able to handle a tense situation. Other decisions about our ability to handle responsibility will be inferred from such a perception.

Male perceptions of women's anger often are irrational too. It is one more challenge of male and female interpersonal relationships in the workplace. Some men find women's anger in the most innocuous of situations–especially if they are looking for it.

Harriet Lerner relates an experience she had while attending a professional conference. "A young doctor," she says, "presented a paper about battered women. She shared many new and exciting ideas and conveyed a deep personal involvement in her subject. In the middle of the presentation a well known psychiatrist, who was seated behind me, got up to leave. As he stood, he turned to the man next to him and made his diagnostic pronouncement: 'Now, that is a very angry woman!'"

Some women we spoke with suggested that when we are angry we should ask ourselves "Can I do anything about this?" If the answer is no, let it go. If the answer is yes, offer a solution and negotiate until you get at least a good part of what you want and need. Anger, they agreed, is effective if you express it, make the point, and go on. It loses its effectiveness if you carry a grudge or never let the bad feelings go. Historically, men have been better at this than women, but women are learning very fast.

The Boss's Anger

And what about your boss's anger? How does a woman successfully deal with that?

You can acknowledge his feelings by saying "I know you're

angry, or "I can see that you are angry." You can express regret
for the anger without accepting blame. Try to understand what
he is saying, and above all don't get defensive. He's still the
boss.

Handling yourself effectively in a difficult situation with
your boss doesn't mean proving that you are right–or even
that he is wrong.

When the boss is angry with you, your goal should be to
diffuse that anger when possible to allow both your ego *and*
his to remain intact. This allows you to move on after the
situation has been resolved.

Anger can, but does not have to, destroy a working relationship.

As in any troubled relationship, there are things that can be
worked out if both parties want to work it out, and things that
can never be agreed on. Jessie Olivier tells us from sad experience that "you can't really ever nail your boss. If you do that,
a reputation will follow you and probably hurt you more than
the boss. If you can't work it out, move on. When the boss
becomes the enemy, you can't win."

Good Bosses

Are there any good bosses? Many women have assured us
there are. For some men being the person in charge means
empowering others. These men like to coach and mentor staff
and have adopted a more open approach to management.

My boss was a wonderful mentor," says Celeste Johns. "He
spent a lot of time teaching me the business. He picked me
from a group of prospects, men and women, and thought I had
the best skills and temperament to handle his company. He
saw my being a woman as advantageous. I guess because it
made our company unique in the field and it also made him
look progressive."

Toby Stens agrees. "My boss had a goal of hiring the best
people he could find. After culling through a group of résumés
and interviewing a cross section of applicants, he chose the

most qualified, able people. He ended up with all the top people in his group being women.

"The partner of the firm and the national office staff noticed that the whole group was female and started calling them 'Fred's princesses.' He didn't like it and we definitely abhorred such comments. It demeaned the group and its efforts. Each woman was very competent and each has gone on to run her own business, or to run a corporation. However, my boss told me specifically that he was told during his performance review that he would not be successful if his next hire was not a male. Can you imagine?"

Yardley Peters adds, "I once went to a meeting with my boss and we both sat quietly during the whole time. When we left I got up the courage to tell him that he was not enthusiastic in that meeting. He said I should have jumped in. I never thought it was my place to do that.

"He said to me, 'if you see something that needs redirection, you should speak up.' Fortunately, we were able to go back and I took a deep breath and offered some additional analysis to the discussion. I think it was my fear of sexism that got in the way and my conditioning to be subservient in a paternalistic environment. I learned a lot from him though. He was wonderful."

Consistently, the traits that were identified in good bosses were an ability to listen, to be considerate, to structure tasks efficiently, to explain responsibilities clearly, to recognize the needs of subordinates and to recognize achievement and effort.

"A bad boss can make your life a living hell," says Stephanie Davies, "and a good one can motivate and inspire you to do things you never believed you could have done. Who your boss is makes all the difference in the world."

In Conclusion

Women should choose their bosses very carefully. It's useful to identify the kinds of support you will need from a boss to advance to where you want to be and to apply this criteria carefully when interviewing a potential boss.

When the male ego consumes a boss it can spell career disaster for an ambitious woman. Coping with difficult interpersonal issues between male bosses and female subordinates can become so draining that productivity suffers.

The women in this chapter shared their experiences in coping with information hoarding, controlling, and hysterical bosses by confronting them, reassuring them, being consistently competent, and refusing to disappear. No single response is considered appropriate for all situations–there is no one right way.

Difficult bosses provoke anger in their subordinates and some women find expressing anger difficult. Anger is an effective response if you can express it, make the point, and go on. Hesitation, indirectness, vacillation, and carrying resentment give others cause not to take you or your anger seriously.

The boss's anger also has to be responded to. The less defensive your response to the boss's anger, the more effective your response will be and the easier it will be to move on.

While egotistical bosses throw stumbling blocks in an ambitious woman's way, good bosses can provide insight and opportunities not readily available from other sources.

The women we spoke with identified the most important qualities to look for in a boss as: an ability to listen, to be considerate, to structure tasks efficiently, to explain responsibilities clearly, to recognize the needs of subordinates, and to recognize achievement and effort.

7

You're in Charge

"When Harvard men say they have graduated from Radcliffe, then we've made it."
    Jacqueline Kennedy Onnasis

*"B*oss" is not a title most men are comfortable ascribing to women. Men used to be afraid to report to a woman. Not so long ago they were sure that reporting to a woman would harm, derail, or stall their careers. It's no secret that the most powerful jobs are still held by men. Men who always worked for other men worried that their status would diminish if they were assigned to a woman.

With the advent of changing demographics most men in the next century will have women bosses randomly throughout their careers. Well educated, prepared, competent women are here to stay.

Many women currently in middle management positions will rise to upper management. Some will attain the positions of CEO and president. Industry can no longer afford to relegate talented women and minorities to second-string jobs. The glass ceiling will have to shatter and diversity will be the way an organization best evolves.

When a man's boss is a woman, his initial response is often that the world has been turned upside down. Women have been the caregivers, teachers, nurses, and mother of his early experience. Concomitantly, his concepts of women as objects and men as superior are reinforced in the most accessible artifacts of our popular culture–movies, books, magazine covers, and television.

Traditionally, men are the gender in control. Being a boss is all about having power. The male model of power implies the ability to have command or authority over others. When a woman has power, it makes some men very nervous. For others, to be commanded and controlled by a woman is not acceptable and leads to resistance.

Matthew Evans was told by a senior partner in his firm that women were not capable of doing certain things simply because they were female. "I have seen women professionals lied to," he says. "I have seen them passed over, I have heard them described in unflattering terms, often simply when they were emulating the behavior of their male counterparts."

Barriers to success are real for women who expect to exert power. The hierarchal structure of organizations, the old boys network, organizational custom, folklore, and prejudice all serve to exclude women. Margaret Shorrisk, a hospital administrator says, "I don't focus on the fact that I am a woman. I try to create neutral ground for negotiating with men. I have great concentration and great interest in what I am doing. I let this drive out the tendency to focus on myself and how others are accepting or not accepting me. Women grow up worrying too much about acceptance. Many times I don't care if they accept me, but I care very much if my position on an issue gets accepted."

Learning to renegotiate the interaction between women and men and to establish equilibrium among the gender issues is the next single great workplace challenge.

Power is a relatively new concept for women. Historically, we have not had much access to it. Its newness often causes the female boss problems. Women are more apt to encounter sexism if they lead in an autocratic way. Some women fear that if they wield power effectively and enjoy it, they risk becoming just like men. They know the road to respect is not the route of imitating men. Sometimes, this sets up a frustrating conflict.

When a boss is conflicted about her own authority, she cannot expect her subordinates to accept that authority without being conflicted themselves.

EDITH

Edith was the CEO of a financial services agency. Her first year there she learned that some men, in an effort to get what they wanted, resorted to the same approaches that worked with the women in their own families.

Ralph, one of Edith's senior deputies, wanted seven members of his staff to receive training in construction finance. Edith knew that in the twenty years of the firm's history it had only made five construction loans. She also knew the recession was easing and construction money was becoming available.

Edith told Ralph to prepare a memo detailing the rationale for his proposal, providing data on which to make a decision and identify prospective customers. Once the research and analysis was completed, Edith promised to discuss his idea. She emphasized that construction loans were a limited practice of the firm. If the decision was to pursue this business, she would only approve training two people. Ralph agreed and they arranged to meet within two weeks.

The next week at the senior staff meeting the training issue was discussed with enthusiasm. Edith reiterated her position, yet Ralph insisted that training as many people as possible was a worthwhile investment.

Later that day, Edith met with Ralph to review his memo. It essentially recommended Ralph's original proposal and ignored Edith's concerns. Edith was quite annoyed. Here was an issue they had discussed. He knew the parameters, yet he was still asking that they train seven people. She repeated her concerns and her direction to limit the number of people who were trained. She asked him why he had not done as he was asked.

Ralph asked Edith if she were calling him insubordinate. Then he burst into tears. He cried.

Edith was stunned. She felt like a bitch and could not fathom what she had done to make a grown man cry. It was certainly nothing over which she would have cried. She just did not think men cried over anything. She felt so upset she could hardly work that day. However, she gave in and let him train five people.

In retrospect, she thought she should have deferred the decision about the training to a time when Ralph was less upset.

Later, when she discussed her reaction to Ralph's tears with her brother, he laughed and confessed that men could play that card, too. He told her she should have told Ralph he could not train anyone. He helped her understand how Ralph had manipulated her and that he would not have cried if his boss had been a man.

If his boss had been a man . . . .

Marilyn Elias is a reporter for *USA Today.* In her May 20, 1991 "Health" column she reported on the proceedings of the 1991 annual meeting of the American Psychological Association. She says that in a workforce survey of over 300 individuals, conducted by a Purdue University psychologist, it was found that:

- Women bosses are most apt to encounter sexism if they lead in an autocratic way.
- Men tend to be judged higher in ability as supervisors.
- Employees are happier reporting to women bosses.

Marilyn Elias reported that men are judged higher in ability as supervisors, yet employees are happier reporting to a woman boss. Why?

Some women told us they view their male bosses as fairer

and more understanding than female bosses. Faye Bramson, a municipal bond trader, says that what she admires about her male boss is his "ability to evaluate people's worth quickly." She says, "He makes decisions about people and then supports those who are capable and drops those who aren't. He's decisive."

If men are perceived as decisive and fair, then why do staff say they are happier reporting to a woman? Calvin Budd, an engineer, was surprised by his own experience.

"My female boss," he says, "was very different from my male boss. She took the time to recognize my work, take me to lunch, and to celebrate the birth of our baby.

"She believed it was important to understand the whole of a person's life including the pressures away from the job. That helped us work out a schedule that was realistic when our babysitter had a crisis and my wife had to go out of town for her job.

"I appreciated her support and I worked extra hard to produce the work she needed. My male boss was only interested in the bottom line. He did say thanks, but he never acknowledged any of the milestones in our lives."

"To be an effective boss, I've found that I've got to care, but not take care of my employees," says Janis Braithwaite, an import-export executive. "It's a hard line to walk. The temptation is always to take care of people. I know I have a strong desire to be liked, and that's a handicap when you're a boss."

Janis is right. To be an effective boss, one must accept the fact that hard decisions are the price one pays for achieving power in an organization. Men know this. A desire to be liked is in direct conflict with the exercise of power.

Harrison Redding, a career naval officer, observes that "sometimes women, especially very young women, have a hard time understanding the difference between being a manager and being a friend. This is a very bad mistake in the workplace.

"I learned this early in my naval career. We were taught as officers to know our people, to know what skills they had, but if we got too personal we were told that we were making ourselves unfit to do our jobs.

"We were told that the subordinate who you allowed to become your friend would be the same man that you would one day have to order into a battle–and maybe to his death. That's a little dramatic, but the point is it affects your judgment. . . . It mixes things up."

The need to be liked sets up relationships that confuse everybody. It may be women's greatest obstacle to becoming topnotch bosses. Inappropriate relationships erode your position as a power figure. Mixed messages are sent and before you know what's happened your employees are holding all the cards. Some first-class manipulation by subordinates has resulted from a boss's inappropriate need to be liked.

SUSAN

Susan supervised five people, four of whom were men. Two of her senior staff were locked in a competitive struggle for her attention. Jack and Tony feared that Susan might regard one as more worthy than the other. Tony saw himself as Jack's equal. Jack worried that Tony might be the better man.

Susan was shocked by their level of pettiness. She knew they were competitive, but the lengths they would go to "stay even" was beyond anything she had ever seen.

When Susan authorized a company car for Jack, Tony insisted he needed one too. When Jack saw Tony with a lap-top computer, he headed straight for Susan's office with the same request. Car phones also were a subject of battle.

Jack would present a cogent argument for why he needed his equipment. Susan would approve the purchases. Then Tony would come into her office and whine about Jack's perks. He always seemed to be able to wear Susan down until she agreed to approve the same item for him.

Susan saw no increase in their productivity as a result of all these added tools. She had the feeling these were not legitimate requests and that she was being caught in the middle of some type of ego game.

The rivalry played out in many ways, including Tony's need to monopolize the conversation during staff meetings. He always tried to appear more knowledgeable than Jack about everything. He was full of bluster and Susan often felt embarrassed for him.

Susan attempted to intervene, but someone's feelings would always be hurt. One or the other of them always felt slighted and the sulking and resentment was irritating.

On the advice of her mentor, Susan hired an organizational psychologist to work with the group. He took one week to make his assessment. "Susan," he said, "you've got to take charge. The tail of this operation is beginning to wag the dog. No matter how much you give in to them, how many times you tell them they are both valuable to the firm, and how many times you try to be fair, nothing will ever be enough for those two.

"You have allowed an impossible situation to develop," he told her. "Use your authority. If they won't be productive, fire one and the one who is left will begin to respect you. I guarantee it."

Susan felt humiliated. "I slipped into acting like their mother," she says. "I dealt with them just the way I deal with my kids at home, and the results were about the same."

In retrospect she says, "When we mother our staff we foster immaturity and they get the message that it is all right to act up and to be immature. Now, when they whine I do nothing to reinforce it. My attitude is the behavior has to change before we can get anywhere. Shape up, or ship out. They understand very clearly."

The kind of trap Susan fell into is not unique when a woman is the boss, nor is it the only kind. Another trap is assuming men need less supervision, especially on technical matters, than women. Remember Jeanette and Dave?

JEANETTE

Jeanette assumed Dave knew what he was doing and, therefore, she gave him a lot of freedom because he was a man and
because he had "done it all before." She admittedly supervised
her female staff more closely. The result was Dave's taking full
advantage of meeting with Jeanette's boss and placing himself
in the limelight. This would not have been so destructive had
Dave's sights not also been set on Jeanette's job.

Jeanette put the brakes on too late. She slipped out of her
supervisory mode and slid into something more familiar–
accepting the male evaluation of the situation as the right one.
It was certainly unconscious, but destructive nevertheless.
She allowed her power to erode. She gave away her authority.
She did not want to anger or hurt her staff member. It was a
rude awakening when Jeanette lost her job.

Never make the mistake of thinking that once you have
"made it" you needn't pay attention to politics. You *never* reach
that point. Politics is a fact of organizational life.

LYDIA

When Lydia assumed the presidency of her company, she
followed the example of her father, a successful entrepreneur.
She researched the company, requested the résumés and performance reviews of all the key staff, and tried to ascertain
who were the most talented employees. She observed and
asked questions aimed at identifying who had perceived
power and who held membership in the old boy's network.
She also reviewed the personnel policies and procedures and
met with groups of staff to establish some rapport, and to hear
from them what were the positive and negative aspects of their
jobs as well as what they liked or what disturbed them about
the company.

She was faced with energizing an entrenched bureaucracy
loyal to her predecessor whose leadership was predominately

male. She knew she had to fire a few people to effect overall efficiency and to establish her authority. Her father once told her that when the conqueror captures a village, a few of the vanquished are banished from the village or shot in the public square so that everyone realizes who is boss.

She brought her own team, notably some top-flight women managers, met with each business unit, reassigned staff, requested postdated resignations of all the senior people, hosted monthly coffee hours, and established workgroups.

The staff that she inherited was on notice that the old ways of doing business held no currency. Although there was much grumbling mixed with awe expressed around the coffeepot, most people were trying to prove their worth.

The business strategy of the company was changing and Lydia wanted the workgroups to analyze the impact of the proposed changes on their respective areas and to recommend options. She used this approach to win ownership around the changes and to increase participation.

Over the years, Lydia had witnessed the fallout from the transition from one CEO to another. Now that it was her turn. She was determined to have people feel part of her organization, to identify a good team, and redeploy those who resisted change. She used the monthly coffee hour as a way to get out amongst her staff and to learn their concerns. She knew from experience that women presidents are not taken as seriously as men. She was determined to win respect, not popularity.

Her first major problem was with George, the publicist who had been with the company eight years. He was not receptive to Lydia's point of view and would disagree often. Lydia noted that he would clench his fists and talk in clipped tones in response to her directions. He insisted on speaking for her and interpreting to the staff her wishes, as if to give her requests legitimacy or credibility. He would argue with Lydia about her approach and try to minimize her thinking. The company was being positioned as a market leader, which meant their public relations and advertising postures had to be revamped. George resisted the change and Lydia's direction. When he continued to undermine her decisions and to bend her requests, she fired him.

George was furious. He did not believe he had been fired. He went directly to the chairperson of the corporation for clarification. The board chairperson assured George that Lydia had the authority to fire him. George could not understand how this young woman could run the company and not do as he suggested. After all, he had been at the company for many years and she was just so new to the business. The board chair wondered if Lydia had been a young man if George would have had a similar problem. George insisted it was not the same thing. The board chair thanked George for his service and reminded him this was a new day. George had to learn to take direction from a female boss.

Max, a senior department head, did not seem to be able to handle the analytic demands the new business focus required. Lydia asked her human resources person to assess his performance to see if they could locate another spot for him. He had been with the company seventeen years and had made a significant contribution. His retirement was only two years off and security was very important to him. After some mutual exploration, Max and the human resources staff agreed that the purchasing department was where his skills–attention to detail and follow through–could be utilized better.

In a matter of months, Lydia had established her style and authority in the company. She began immediately to address the new directions of the corporation and to build some ownership around the process through a network of company-wide workgroups. She fired a few people, reassigned others, and dislodged the bureaucracy by moving people around; thereby, loosening the traditional communications links. She tried to balance her concerns for the organization and her concern for its people. Her need for affiliation was met through the support of a core group of staff with whom she worked and for whom she hoped to set a positive example.

Arturo Bolla spoke of his boss with pride. "Whenever I saw our CEO run a meeting she behaved like a competent manager," he says. "It was incidental that she was a woman. The men treated her with the utmost respect."

BETTE

Bette was the newly hired controller who had inherited Gerald, a senior accountant. He had good performance reviews, yet it was not clear to her how he had managed to receive acceptable ratings from her predecessor. She discovered that he did not know how to handle even the most routine functions of his job.

"When I was trying to find out how Gerald was coming along with a project, I would ask, 'How much have you done? When will you finish?' He would say, 'Let me ask you something, you don't like me do you?' I would say, 'That is not the point, we need this work completed by such and such a time and I need to know when we can expect it.'"

He always tried to personalize any instruction or criticism. He accused her of not understanding him and complained she was not fair to male staff. Bette dealt with each of his complaints directly and confronted him about their personality differences. She remained firm, however, a certain standard of work was required.

Bette discerned he needed some additional training, but Gerald refused to acknowledge that need and would not participate in any staff development or training activities. His pride would not allow him to ask for help from a woman. Finally, she had to let him go.

FIONA

Fiona supervised a group of five people, three men and two women. Both women had a problem with Leonard who felt he had to protect the younger women.

Initially, Fiona had to mediate disputes between Leonard

and his female colleagues. Leonard would usurp their pre-rogatives or appropriate their responsibilities. He saw himself as omniscient. They viewed him as patronizing, pompous, and presumptuous in his relationships with women. When the women confronted him, he always had some excuse that reflected his belief that he was being helpful, or was saving them from a harsh experience. He never seemed to hear their complaint. They were always so angered by his patronizing explanations that they did not hear his point.

Individually, Fiona coached the women to respond to Le-onard's discussion and evaluation of their mutual work plans and to ignore the putdowns. She allowed them to vent their frustration to her. She made it clear to Leonard that he would be evaluated on development and teamwork. She asked him to construct some measures around these goals. Leonard re-sented the possibility of losing points for what he viewed as helpful behavior.

Whenever he frustrated one of his colleagues by trying to manage her area or intervene in her process, Fiona reviewed with all of them the impact of his behavior on the group's morale and on the staff's shared work plan. It took a year of Fiona's persistence and lost points on his performance review before Leonard was willing to change.

Eventually, after a series of meetings where all the parties came together around their concerns, Leonard learned to work more effectively with his colleagues. The women learned to deal with the matters at hand and not to reinforce Leonard's ego-driven behavior.

MARCIA

Marcia, a nurse administrator at a teaching hospital, remem-bered how she and a chief of service helped a "temperamental" surgeon do his job. The surgeon was arrogant, rude, and abusive toward the nursing staff. He behaved like a superhero, did not like to be questioned, would explode at the drop of a hat, and demanded that all the staff, especially the women, serve him.

The surgeon's work was brilliant and valued by patients and colleagues. His behavior was problematic, especially for the hospital managers who wanted to stabilize the nursing staff and did not want any of the physicians making life untenable for them.

After months of vociferous complaints and several grievances, Marcia and the surgeon's chief of service worked out a solution. First, they met with the nursing staff to hear their suggestions for solving this problem. Then they met with the surgeon and shared the complaints and grievances. They told him the staff would not tolerate his behavior and that continued complaints would result in his loss of hospital privileges, that is, his dismissal.

Together, they focused on the physician's behavior and decided the chief would be the primary person to handle the physician's complaints or requests. Marcia was charged with making sure her staff collaborated and referred the physician to the chief rather than engage in a struggle with him.

To reinforce this decision, Marcia notified the chief whenever the surgeon was scheduled to operate. The chief went to the floor or called the surgeon to see how things were going. He handled all the surgeon's requests and tried to make sure he had what he needed.

Marcia and the chief served as buffers and worked together to preserve the relationships by setting boundaries for the staff and limiting the surgeon's opportunities to act out.

Women Bosses

Edith, Susan, Lydia, Bette, Fiona, and Marcia join a host of women who have an opportunity to forge a variety of new models for motivating and managing people. Now, many managers are working to achieve cooperation and commitment rather than control and compliance. Women are socialized to incorporate cooperation and commitment into their value systems. Indeed, these are part of the female armamentarium of strengths and are expressed in the ways they build their family relationships and webs of social supports. Creating an environment that taps the best in people is part of a woman's social development, and is a well practiced skill most readily seen in doll play in childhood, later in women's interactions with children, and around staff development processes in the workplace.

Working in lower level jobs and being in subordinate workplace roles has meant that women have had to observe and study what was happening around them to survive. Reaching the top of an organizational structure has meant that women have had to overcome bias and barriers. Women who are bosses are as objective and analytical as their male counterparts. These abilities are enhanced by an underpinning of having learned to develop a deeply rooted connection to the people in their world. Once in power women have the opportunity to abandon the male model of command, control, hierarchy, and to invent alternative approaches to manage others through empowerment.

In Conclusion

"Instead of accepting the notion of power as dominion, mastery, or power over, feminist researchers propose an alternative model of interaction stressing power with or power from emerging interaction. Through mutual empowerment, rather than competition, a context is created and sustained which increases understanding and moves participants to joint action. This model overrides the active/passive dichotomy and calls for interaction among all participants in the relationship to build connection and enhance everyone's power."

This model was discussed by Deborah Kolb and Gail Coolidge in their 1991 article, "Her Place at the Table: A Consideration of Gender Issues in Negotiation." It reflects women's predisposition to talk through a problem, consider the voices of many when issues arise, and attempt to accommodate the needs of others. Several women executives shared how they saw their roles as "working for" their direct reports to facilitate the goals and accomplishments of each person and as brokering the interests of their workgroups with their superiors. These women felt it was their job to help maximize the contributions of their workgroups and to create an environment where each felt empowered. Rose's goal was to build a cooperative, rather than a competitive, team to work through her project. Lydia organized her workforce into small workgroups to think through new organizational changes. Marcia tried to preserve a relationship rather than dispense with one.

The rewards for exercising power in new and alternative ways are different and often yield better results. Executives see their employees grow, develop, and become more self-directed. Subordinates take more responsibility for their productivity, contribute their ideas, and have a greater sense of ownership when a process has included their insights. Problem solving by talking through issues allows more openness and greater opportunity for creative resolutions. When those with whom you work feel your support and hear your supportive voice, they work harder to solve the tough issues, smooth the bruised relationships, generate innovation, and produce definitive reports. Their talents and efforts reflect well on you and provide you with what you need to look good for your superiors. Everyone wins.

8

Becoming Colleagues

"The first problem for all of us, men and women, is not to learn, but to unlearn."

Gloria Steinem

The Rising Star

"When a woman behaves like a man," Dame Edith Evans once asked, "Why doesn't she behave like a nice man?"

Dame Edith must have met Audrey. Audrey was the first female member of the management team of the new products division of a large insurance company. Bright, ambitious, assertive, she had confidence in her abilities and was willing, even anxious, to do whatever was asked of her to be successful.

Audrey knew she was in a highly visible spot, and she was determined not to make any mistakes. No one was going to take advantage of her because she was a woman. Audrey would be as tough as any of the men. She wouldn't give them any reason to think she could be manipulated.

When her senior actuary gave a lackluster presentation to the management group, she attacked him publicly. When her boss criticized the same employee's work on another project, she fired him without saying a word to anyone. He sued and the company became embroiled in a legal battle.

When her colleagues teased her about it, she turned on them. "I just did what none of you would have had the guts to do," she said. "This is just the beginning. I'm getting rid of all the deadwood in my area."

While they joked about her and called her "Macha" behind her back, the other managers felt more and more uncomfortable with Audrey. She challenged them openly and continuously at meetings. She criticized them to the boss behind their backs. She missed no opportunity to make herself look good at their expense.

Audrey's eye was always focused on the boss. If her subordinates made an error she thought made her look bad she exercised no mercy.

Her male colleagues avoided her, which only increased her anger. She complained to the boss that they refused to cooperate with her because she was a woman. He was initially sympathetic because her area was so productive, but as her productivity declined, due to the high turnover rate and poor morale of her staff, he became less and less patient with her. He told her she needed to repair her relationships if she expected to continue working for the firm.

What was Audrey thinking of? She was smart, ambitious, and willing. She was aggressive and the equal of any of her male colleagues. She knew the value of visibility, decisiveness, and of "playing hard ball." She thought she had succeeded in creating a level playing field.

Audrey was a dynamo, but she never learned to be a colleague. She never learned that one requirement for becoming a team captain is that you play on the team.

Team Work

"It may be logical to assume that performance is the only real criteria for success," says David Metcalf, a retired public relations executive, "but you can be the best performer in the world and still get nowhere. Excellence is only one factor. You have to work with other people–cooperate, compete, and negotiate. You can't play the game by ignoring the rules and then hope to win."

Audrey believed that "proving herself" was all that mattered. She lost focus on the need to become collaborative and supportive. Ultimately she added no value and left a trail of unhappy subordinates, frustrated colleagues, and a lawsuit for someone else to clean up.

Audrey discounted one of women's greatest strengths in the workplace–the ability to be an effective member of a working team. She copied those angry traits of the male ego–that need to control others and succeed at their expense. It worked no better for Audrey than it does for men who continue to use it.

"Women," says social worker Ira Greene, "naturally incline toward inclusiveness. Generally, women prefer to reach decisions by consensus and to resolve problems through a series of negotiated adjustments. They are naturals at collaborative work.

"Men and women approach teamwork differently," he says, "but all seem to value a team approach. What I mean is, men will support each other, work together, without much conversation but with everyone's eyes on the goal–in the way sports team members play. Women, on the other hand, prefer more communication and interaction among the team members.

"To men, the goal is more important than any of the individual players. For women, it seems the opposite is true."

There is no one best approach as long as the job gets done. What matters in any corporation or institution is the task and the team. Some team members are motivated by the leader's interest in them while others prefer a leader who maintains more distance. Whichever leader can motivate his or her particular staff to a successful outcome is the winner.

Maternalism

Women may have an edge in the cooperative teamwork arena, but they have to be careful to maintain a balance. "We may be excellent nurturers and champions of cooperation," says Dana Cole, an airline executive, "but we must never fall into the trap of becoming the mothers of the workplace. It is incumbent on females to help men understand that we are not their mothers.

"We have to take the initiative here. We have to stop allowing ourselves to be Mother Confessor to our male colleagues. When they come by to talk make sure you talk about the work, your goals, and the business. You've got to insist on maintaining an equal footing. Women's attitudes must drive this change. Always be clear on who you are and what is appropriate."

"Maternalism does not belong in the workplace," says Charles Davies, a public administrator for city government. "Gender issues should not upset the balance in the colleague-to-colleague relationship."

"There's a more practical issue here," adds Nora, a freelance fashion designer. "I think high powered, creative women tend to take a motherly approach with their staff and with other members of their team. It seems to me that it's an attempt to ensure loyalty from the people who work for or with them. Men intimidate to build loyalty but women mother.

"It's a dangerous style for everybody. If the mothering backfires the result, in my experience, is rage. The caring mother becomes this incredible bitch. You've got to remember that the "children" will, and do, take advantage of "Mom." When this happens on the job women turn on themselves and on the people who have taken advantage of them. The whole thing gets pretty ugly."

Colleague-to-Colleague

The colleague-to-colleague relationship can be difficult even under the best circumstances. In any organization colleagues vie with each other for territory, power, and promotions. They talk behind each other's backs, overreact to each other, and try to be a hero at the other's expense.

On the positive side, colleagues also have been known to

protect each other from the wrath or deviousness of other colleagues. Even this has problem potential, however. When colleagues are also friends the temptation is often to put the friendship first. If you find yourself making decisions that are designed to keep you in the good graces of your colleague-friend, then you are playing with the dynamite that has blasted the success of countless women in the workplace–the need to be liked first and to be competent second.

Finally, some colleagues band together in support groups to complain about the boss, the company, their salaries, office politics–anything to take the heat off themselves. Gripe sessions are good places to rationalize your behavior while getting support for blaming everyone else–at least everyone not present. This relieves stress temporarily, but the benefit deteriorates rapidly.

Negativity is contagious. Misery loves company–and often will make it hard for "company" to leave the circle of complainers. Joining the ranks of the chronic malcontents in an organization can be the beginning of career suicide for you.

While all of us complain from time to time about how hard it is being a boss, or having a boss, being a colleague is tough too. Every major problem we encounter in the workplace can be traced in one form or another to interpersonal struggles. Although it is true that it takes two to create an interpersonal difficulty or, as your mother probably told you, "you can't fight with yourself." The range of extraordinarily difficult personalities one encounters in the workplace might make Mom reconsider.

The Bully, the Equivocator, and the Distractor are colleagues who could test Mother Teresa's generosity. Unfortunately, they are as much a part of our worklife as our desk, our computer, and our paycheck.

The Bully

The Bully surely is the most frustrating of this problem trio. You can't embarrass the Bully by calling him on his behavior–he likes to be viewed as a threat. It makes him feel powerful and in control. The Bully is arrogant and intimidating. It is never enough for him to be right. Everybody around him must be wrong.

You might have guessed that the Bully is an overgrown, spoiled child. While the rest of civilization is looking for appropriate ways to release the creativity of their "inner child" this monster freely inflicts his "inner brat" on anyone unfortunate enough to get in his way! He is convinced that his needs are more important than anyone else's and he expects his staff and co-workers to understand that.

"Bullies are not sympathetic figures, but most lead very unhappy lives," says social worker Ira Greene. "They have an overwhelming need to control the events around them. Bullies can't ask for help. They are terrified of looking foolish or incompetent. They will question the competence and motivation of their colleagues just to take the focus off themselves."

Lillie Reed is a New York City Housing Authority police officer who says she has worked with and around bullies for the last ten years. Lillie says, "You can't allow a bully to make you look bad. You don't have to make him look bad—bullying a bully usually doesn't work—but you do have to stay calm and not engage in his foolishness.

"Bullies would like you to feel obligated to them." She adds, "Don't buy into that. You're not wrong, or responsible, or stupid just because he says you are. Bullies are great actors. You know what—you can act too. Pretend his opinion doesn't matter—even if it does. Don't follow his program.

"Bullies," says Lilly, "are little boys. Grown men don't have to knock people around to get their attention."

Debra Truax is the comptroller of a computer software firm. She deals on a daily basis with the directors of marketing, sales, and research and development. All three of these managers have different requirements from the finance department and the way they request what they need reflects three very different interpersonal styles.

The director of marketing is a negotiator. He's not terribly comfortable dealing with the intricacies of budgeting, responding to monthly variance reports, or projecting year-end costs, so he has worked out a system with Debra's staff that suits them all. They have adapted the reporting system to his work cycle, and they have trained his deputy director to maintain it.

The director of research and development is a well organized individual–a perfectionist. Debra has no problem with him. If every process was twice as complicated and cumbersome he'd still get his figures in a day early.

The director of sales is another story. Evan is a man in a hurry who just can't be bothered with detail. He views his division as "the guys who bring in the money." It is, he believes, the responsibility of the support areas–accounting, purchasing, data processing, and personnel–to support him and stay out of his way.

Evan tramples all over the internal systems of the company. He criticizes Debra and the other support directors openly at meetings and to his sales force. He encourages his subordinates to work around systems and procedures, to ignore them and if problems arise to "call him" and he will "take care of it." Evan is a bully.

Evan is late with every sales report. He holds up production of the organization's statistics, sales analysis, and monthly closings on a regular basis. No one stops him. Evan and the president "grew up in the company" and the unspoken message is that Evan is to be accommodated.

Evan's manner is arrogant and abrasive. While all the support areas suffer, he seemed to save his special venom for finance. Evan drones on at staff meetings and in public forums that the finance department is incompetent, doesn't understand the business, and can't deliver what sales needs. Evan, however, can never be specific about just what it is sales needs. Debra suspects that Evan doesn't know.

Evan is also unapproachable. When Debra asked for a list of the reports he wanted, he brushed her off. "Never mind," he said sarcastically, "your guys will only screw it up anyway."

Debra dealt with Evan's bullying by absorbing the blows and keeping her staff out of his way for three years. It was exhausting.

124 COPING WITH THE MALE EGO IN THE WORKPLACE

Then a new president was appointed. He began to demand more timely reporting and better analysis from Evan. Evan began to sweat. When he blamed Debra for not providing him support, the president asked Evan what he needed that he was not able to get. Evan had no answer. He had no idea.

"This is your responsibility," the new president said, "and your performance had better improve."

The other support directors grabbed the opportunity to complain about Evan's style. The president, feeling no special loyalty to Evan, explained that those in senior management who could not support a collegial managerial style would be replaced.

It took everything Evan had and two meetings for him to ask for Debra's help. The first meeting began with Evan's justifying himself and sniping at her. She got up and walked out. It felt wonderful.

The second meeting was more productive. Debra assigned the assistant comptroller the task of orienting Evan to the systems he had criticized so openly in the past. He also had abused the assistant comptroller who now took great delight in the revelation that Evan didn't understand the first thing about budgeting or sales analysis. Debra wondered who had covered him for so long. She suspected it was his former mentor–the old president. Evan was going through a humiliating process, but it was hard for her to feel sorry for him.

Debra was, in fact, surprised by the extent of her rage. She was so disturbed by her feelings that she went to speak about them with Tom Lyons the vice president for human resources. "I'm surprised at myself," she said. "I don't want him to succeed. He's asking for help and I want to rub his face in it.

"I always thought if he just gave a little I'd meet him half way, but I guess this just went on too long. He doesn't feel any differently toward me. It's just that he's on the ropes right now. But if he ever got into a power position again, he'd go right back to being a bastard."

Tom understood Debra's position, but he counseled her against cutting off her own professional nose in the process of spiting his arrogant face. "Evan's a sales powerhouse," he said. "If you two can hammer out a relationship, both you and the company will benefit–so will our profit sharing fund!"

Debra was uncomfortable. "There's nothing left to build a relationship on," she said. "I'm too angry. I feel like I'm being used."

"Well," said Tom, "on the other hand, even if nothing changes you know you can survive. You've been doing it for three years and you coped, you got through. It wasn't pleasant and it took a lot of energy, but you got your work done, and you were successful."

The option of doing nothing had never occurred to Debra. The notion that she had come through despite Evan had never occurred to her either. The choices were not simply helping Evan or telling him to go to hell. She had another option. She could just sit back and watch. Evan's larger-than-life arrogance had dominated the landscape for so long that Debra automatically responded to his behavior. That was no longer necessary. It was not her problem. She did not have to fix it.

Permission to do nothing seemed to relieve Debra's debilitating anger. She met with Evan the following morning and told him she thought they might be able to work together for the good of the firm despite the fact they did not like each other. She told him that if he ever abused her or any member of her staff again, however, she would cut him off. Her voice was calm as she told him, "I know how to make you look bad. Push me and I will. I've got nothing to lose.

"When you deal with bullies," Debra says in retrospect, "what you accept, you teach."

Evan didn't make it, but it was not through any action of Debra's. The assurance that Tom had given her helped her grow as a colleague and as a boss. It was someone just like himself who finally tripped Evan up and got him fired," Debra says. "Now I've got him to deal with, but I'm not worried, I've learned how to do it."

The Equivocator

Bullies like Evan are difficult to deal with, however, Equivocators are another breed of blood pressure elevator. Equivocators must be liked by everyone. Rather than risk rejection they will commit to schedules they know they can never keep, and will tell only half the story if the other half is unpleasant. "Good Old Larry" was just such an Equivocator. Everybody loved Larry. Larry played Father Confessor at the video production company where Sara Winfield worked as personnel director. Larry was responsible for inventory and distribution. Larry had a heart of gold, and everyone agreed. Larry could not bear to hurt or offend anyone. He had a reputation for "smoothing things over" at work. When employees got into trouble with the boss, Larry could be counted on to advocate for them. He could always "find a way" to get help for someone–even if he bent the rules a little to do it.

Although he knew it was against company policy for supervisors to lend money to their staff, Larry did it "on the sly." "People," he said, "are more important to me than regulations."

So, it was not unusual when Larry asked Sara if there was any way he could hire his inventory manager's daughter to work as a secretary in the stockroom. "She's had problems in the past," Larry said. "She's trying to straighten out, and she's got two small kids to support. Jerry has gone into debt paying for her therapy."

Sara reviewed the personnel policy with Larry. Theirs was a family-owned and operated business. The rules were very clear about relatives reporting to relatives. "Maybe we'll be able to find something else for her in another department when things open up a bit," she offered.

Larry smiled. "It's a silly rule," he said. "She's motivated and would do a great job. And Jerry's been with us more than fifteen years."

"I'd like to help," Sara offered, "but you know how management feels about family reporting to family."

"Well, I'd never put you in a difficult position," Larry said. "Let's see what we can do . . . ."

Sara was confused by this remark, but she let it go.

Larry really didn't want to make Sara uncomfortable, but he

didn't want to say no to Jerry either. Larry was an Equivocator of the first order.

Since Jerry and his daughter had different last names and since no one had ever seen her, Larry made the hire. He figured he had covered all the bases. No one could blame Sara, the rule made no sense anyway, and he could help Jerry out.

This mission of mercy landed them all in court. One of Jerry's other employees filed a grievance charging that Jerry favored his daughter over the rest of the staff when it came to overtime distribution. She was let go after six months on the job. She, in turn, filed a lawsuit charging that "management," as represented by Larry, was well aware of her relationship to Jerry when the offer of employment was made.

The suit cost the company plenty. Jerry's daughter won.

What could Sara have done differently? How does one deal successfully with an infuriating Equivocator whose only aim is to "help"?

Whether it is freelancing with policy like this, or agreeing to terms and timelines he knows he can never deliver—just because he can't tell you no—the Equivocator causes plenty of ulcers in the workplce.

"Equivocators," says Judy Chappa, a psychiatric social worker, "are masters at indirect communication. Once you find yourself dealing with this evasive type my advice to you is to listen very, very carefully."

Larry's remark about not wanting to put Sara in a difficult position, followed by his reference to "seeing what could be done," should have triggered a warning bell in Sara's head. It confused her, but she did not pursue it.

In his own mind Larry was letting Sara in on his plan, while at the same time protecting her. He was setting himself up to be the benefactor AND the protector—so like an Equivocator!

"Keep asking for clarification," says Judy. "Keep asking what he means by what he just said. Never ask him what he's going to do. He won't tell you anyway.

"It can be exhausting to work with an equivocator, but if you have no choice, then learn to ask and to listen," Judy says.

"Ask yourself: What is he saying? What is he leaving out? What is his body language trying to tell me?

"It's also a good idea to listen to his jokes and to his good natured teasing for hidden messages. Be patient. It's not that he doesn't want to be direct. He can't be. It's too anxiety provoking for him. Don't wait for him to change. He won't. Don't think you can count on him because he seems like a nice guy—you can't."

The Distractor

The Distractor. Who is he? The Distractor is the guy who blames his problems on everyone else. He's the guy who tells his staff, "If it was up to me you'd all get raises—it's the man in the corner office who's the stumbling block."

The Distractor knows how to keep the heat off himself. He is a master staller. He knows if you just wait long enough decisions either make themselves or someone else will jump in and make them. That suits him fine.

The Distractor will set brush fires all over the organization to keep attention away from himself. He will involve himself in areas where he does not belong, criticize functions he knows nothing about, and when all else fails he has been known to begin rumors.

The Distractor loves to offer you "the bait." "The bait" is a comment or a criticism meant to infuriate you. The goal is a fight. It is always a fight about a minor issue designed to get your attention distracted from the real issue.

The most skilled distractors keep the heat off themselves by asking loaded questions. Tom Drayton was a shop steward in an auto plant in Michigan. He was not terribly popular with the men because he had been unable to stop the union from raising dues twice in eighteen months. Tom needed an issue to get the focus off his own performance. Management unknowingly provided him with that opportunity.

An open meeting was scheduled that afternoon for the men to meet the newest member of the personnel department, Lois Woods, a labor relations specialist. Tom had done a little homework on Lois. She had worked in two auto plants before coming to this one and had successfully defeated a union campaign in one and achieved decertification of an existing union in the other.

No sooner had the personnel director introduced Lois than Tom asked with a disarming smile, "Isn't it true Ms. Woods, that the company recruited you because of your reputation as a union buster?

"The answer, " says Lois, "was clearly 'no.' I was not a union buster and had done nothing illegal. Tom put me off guard however, and I began to explain and rationalize . . . . I started looking pretty guilty, and pretty foolish. About half way through I lost the men. They were suspicious of me, and Tom was clearly their hero again. He is a very skillful man."

A clear, direct "no" would have helped Lois combat Tom's distracting tactics. Focus and clarity work against distractors.

Conflict

Arnold Jarvis is an organization development specialist for a major oil company. Arnold observes that there are three "fuelers" that feed conflict among colleagues. He identifies them as expectation, insult, and retaliation.

"Like the three monkeys in the 'Hear-No-Evil, See-No-Evil, Speak-No-Evil' statue," Arnold says, "one must develop the ability to periodically go blind to expectation, deaf to insult, and dumb to retaliation if you want to minimize conflict.

"Let go of your expectations regarding the behavior of other people," says Arnold. "Ask directly for what you want and accept that sometimes people will come through and sometimes they won't. It has very little to do with you personally.

"Be clear about insults too," he adds. "Tell the person what it is he or she has said that upset you. Ask for amends. If you get them, fine. It may have been an honest misunderstanding. If you don't and the abuse continues, move away from that person. Don't let him become a constant irritant.

"And finally," says Arnold, "avoid retaliation. If you've given a person the opportunity to explain or apologize and he refuses, let it go. Get on with your own work. This, I admit, is easier said then done, but remember it is retaliation and vindictiveness that keep the engines of conflict humming."

Coping with Conflict–Left Brain Style

While conflict is a constant, it can be managed and coped with effectively.

Women can take heart from the Japanese Ninjutsu tradition that approaches conflict resolution in what some have called a "feminine way." Women have been accused of fearing conflict. Critics charge that they avoid it at all costs–including the cost of giving in. True, women do not process conflict in the ways that men do. Avoidance, however, does not always translate into fear. Sometimes it is an expression of good sense. Everyone is uncomfortable with conflict to some degree, and it is no one's first choice.

Japanese businessmen find it very acceptable to avoid conflict when they can, and this position does not seem to have damaged their success drive. The Japanese language has nineteen ways of saying "no." One may be either let down, put down, or knocked down by a well chosen word in that language. In Eastern culture it is accepted that when conflict does arise mutual adjustment is the desired outcome.

Women, who have been trained from toddlerhood to be peacemakers, to share, and to "play nice" suddenly find themselves (ironically) in good company with Ninjutsu masters. It is a new world indeed.

Ninjutsu is a personal survival system. In contrast to the Western tradition of the warrior who is a fighting man, the Ninja warrior is an individual who willingly seeks out the challenges of living.

The Ninja philosophy encourages sensitizing oneself to be able to perceive danger as it approaches rather than to wait to respond once it arrives.

For example, in a conflict the person who is on the attack usually believes strength is the only way to win. The smart opponent, according to Ninja tradition is the one who simply refuses to exhaust himself in a struggle.

Instead of allowing oneself to be lured into battle, the Ninja puts himself in a position where he will be protected from oncoming blows. Precise timing is his weapon. Through subtle shifts the Ninja uses the attacker's own strength against him. Constant shifting puts the attacker off balance. He literally trips over himself.

The secret to success, say Ninjutsu students, is to keep attention focused on the goal. Solid advice no doubt, but how does it work in practice.

Denise is an employee relations specialist for a large commercial bank.

She received numerous complaints from the employees in the accounting department that the comptroller was going through their desks after hours and taking their work, holding it until the next morning, and then criticizing them for the way they were doing it.

"I don't think he has a right to go through our desks," complained the accounts payable supervisor. "I have some private things in my desk that I don't want him looking at."

"I don't think he should feel free to evaluate our work before we're ready to submit it," said the budget manager. "He has no business evaluating my working papers."

Denise spoke with the comptroller who was hostile and defensive. "This operation is crucial to the bank," he said tensely. "I need access to my staff's work. I have a right and a responsibility to know what's going on." Nothing Denise suggested was acceptable to him.

Denise's boss, the personnel director, was no help either. He wanted to remain on good terms with the comptroller and defended his position. A true Equivocator, he told Denise privately that this was not "a hill to die on."

Still, the accountants continued to complain and Denise was frustrated by the lack of respect the comptroller showed for them. Denise counseled them to clearly label the drawers that contained work and those which contained private property.

They did as she suggested, but they continued to find that their desks had been violated.

Denise then helped the staff write a joint memo to the

comptroller reviewing their actions in labeling the drawers and requesting that the drawers labeled "personal" not be opened.

When this was ignored, Denise finally advised them to call security to report desk tampering and the possibility of theft. The staff called, and security began an investigation. Report after report was taken by the security chief.

The comptroller was livid and the personnel director, Denise's boss was furious. The security chief warned the comptroller that what he was doing was a clear violation of bank policy. He asked why the staff hadn't complained to the personnel department instead of wasting his time. He said if he was called again he'd get the chief operating officer involved.

In the true spirit of a Ninjutsu warrior, Denise realized there is more than one way to deal with conflict. Faced with a controlling male ego that was infringing on the rights of others, given her responsibility to address employee relations issues, and given the reluctance of her boss to support her in any meaningful action, she had to find another way.

The comptroller believed the strength of his resistance and the weakness of Denise's boss would enable him to prevail. Denise, who was a smart opponent, refused to allow herself to be drawn into a hopeless battle. She was not about to exhaust herself over this issue.

Denise remained focused on her goal. Since requests, appeals, and all attempts at compromise failed at her level she simply bumped her problem up to the security chief. She subtly reframed the issue from invasion of privacy to possible theft and let security take it on.

And security did. The security chief asked the obvious questions: Why was the comptroller breaching policy, and why wasn't the personnel director doing something about it?

Denise merely allowed her opponent to become entangled in his own resistance. She stepped aside and the problem got solved.

Stephen K. Hayes, an American authority on Ninja tradition, observes, "The goal is ever the attainment of true economy and naturalness in motion, and the ability to let go of inefficient methods."

In Conclusion

Every major problem we encounter in the workplace can be traced in one form or another to interpersonal struggles. There is no way to avoid our responsibility to interact and cooperate with our colleagues. No one in today's workplace has the luxury of remaining a solo artist.

Difficult colleagues make work assignments painful and frustrating. There is never one right way to handle a challenging situation. Because of this, it is critical to develop a variety of interpersonal responses so that you always have a fallback strategy. The women in this chapter learned to cope with the egos of bullies, equivocators, and distractors by confronting, letting go, being focused, and refusing to take the bait. An ability to periodically go blind to expectation, deaf to insult, and dumb to retaliation is also helpful.

Some collegial relationships develop naturally and positively from a foundation of mutual respect. Others are impeded by ego issues and have to be hammered out through interpersonal struggles. Successful styles of conflict resolution can be learned, however, and they become more effective with repeated use.

9

When He's Your Client

"A man has to be Joe McCarthy to be called ruthless.
All a woman has to do is put you on hold."

Marlo Thomas

"Hitters"

*G*race Riley is franchise manager for a nationwide chain of employment agencies. She has been in the business for six years. Grace likes what she does.

"A few months ago," Grace says, "I was working with a potential client who came to speak with us about setting up a franchise for health care recruitment. It was a specialty we ordinarily did not promote. Our business is geared to clerical and financial support staff.

"He was persistent however, and creative, and after a few preliminary meetings with the franchise team it was agreed that we would back him. At that point he officially became a client. Because this was not a routine set up, I personally took his account.

"We went out to dinner and for two hours I talked about the recruitment business, franchising, and start-up operations while he took notes. He really appeared to be listening. I believed he sincerely wanted my advice. It was professionally flattering.

"When dinner was over he said he would walk me home. I lived in the city at that time and the restaurant was about three blocks from my apartment. He walked me to my building and asked if he could come up. I said no. I was beginning to feel uncomfortable.

"Then the other shoe dropped. He told me he had found out that I was newly divorced. He said he was a good listener and a warm person and he could be 'persuaded' to serve as a 'sexual bridge' for me as I coped with my divorce. I thought it was a joke, but he was very serious. He told me he had done this for other women. Of course he was married.

"I couldn't believe it. I felt so stupid. I just said it was late and walked away from him. In the morning I reassigned him to one of my male franchise developers. He went on to purchase the franchise, develop it along the lines he proposed, and he became very successful. We never spoke again. I'm sure he's already forgotten the incident. I don't think I ever will.

"I was in a position to reassign my client to someone else. Many women who work with male clients and customers who sexually pursue them are not able to solve their problems by escape. They have to cope with the situation in other ways.

"If a woman is able to deal with the man who behaves this way and somehow keep the customer, that's winning. It's a tall order, but if she can do it she's won as both a woman and a professional.

Violet Davis, an interior decorator, says that sometimes humor helps. Sometimes by reducing a come-on to a joke, by saying you'd love to call his wife and all have dinner together, or saying you'd be glad to meet him at your boyfriend's apartment, he'll take the hint and not take offense. In that way you allow an inappropriate remark to be played out on another level. Everybody laughs as if it were meant to be a joke from the beginning. You remain in control and you provide him with a graceful exit.

"Honesty also works, if you remain firm," Violet says. "Remember the lines you used when you no longer wanted to date the guy who took you to the prom–'You're a great guy, but I just don't feel that way about you,' 'I'm not interested,' 'I make it a policy never to date clients, and I have never broken that rule–it would make my job too difficult and I won't do it.' But," says Violet, "you must sound firm. You can't say no that sounds like maybe.

"Clients who hit on women are not interested in struggling. Unless you are dealing with a pathological problem, they will give up if they believe there really is no hope. Refuse to be intimidated. Once it is clear that you won't be intimidated, half the fun is gone for the would-be stud.

"He's got a job to do too. He needs whatever service it is you provide. Once you've made yourself clear you can go on with business. He'll look elsewhere, and you'll more than likely keep the account."

The Dilemma

What role could possibly provide more fertile ground for the "male ego" to flourish in than as client or customer?

We've defined this male ego we try to cope with in so many areas of the workplace as the posture meant to intimidate and humiliate. This is the ego that attempts to keep others in inferior or disadvantaged positions to compensate for feelings of insecurity. This is the ego with an overwhelming need to feel superior and in control.

There are mechanisms in the workplace to file grievances against a boss who becomes difficult or to discipline a difficult subordinate–intervention can also be made when one experiences tough interpersonal problems with colleagues. But what can women do when the problem is the client?

Customers and clients are the reason an organization stays in business. If they are not satisfied there won't be a business. Both women and men can feel like tightrope walkers in their attempt to satisfy customers without compromising themselves.

Nancy Cristman loves to talk about her dealings with clients. "I try to maintain a sense of humor," she says, "but it's a struggle." Nancy is an auditor for a large accounting firm. Her business takes her in and out of many of the major corporations in New York, Chicago, and Los Angeles. "The stress can get outrageous," she says.

"One client persists in referring to me as the 'audit gal.' I've approached him several times in what I thought was a tactful way about how offensive this is, but he doesn't get it. Men sometimes don't understand when they offend a woman. The very fact that I confront him is greeted with amusement. This is a further insult.

"This man has a tendency to be overly chummy with me, overly friendly. There is nothing sexual about his behavior, it's more paternalistic. He thinks that a young woman auditor is a novelty. He wouldn't think the same thing about a young man.

"My fantasy is that the next time he refers to me as the 'audit gal,' I'll refer to him as the 'fat middle aged client.' It's one option. It would cost me my job, but I can dream. My real options are either to deal with it and try to keep things in perspective, or to request to be taken off the account. He'll never get it."

"The real boss is the customer," says Martina Wells a merchandising manager. "If you don't believe that the customer is always right, then you'd better get used to acting as if you did. No matter how good you are, if you alienate customers you will ultimately lose your job."

Letty Costello, a nursing supervisor agrees. "Nurses," she says, "have traditionally played a subservient role to physicians. Many women in the profession today resent this and refuse to propagate it. The most unhappy members of my staff are those who never figure out a way to work with this kind of inflated ego. It takes a lot of flexibility and compromise.

"I am not saying they are wrong. Dealing with those egos would give anyone reason to be angry and resentful. I'm only saying they are very unhappy.

"I try to communicate to the nurses that in a hospital, as in any other organization, survival is defined as 'customer service' for both the 'internal' and 'external' customer. In the hospital the physician is the 'internal customer' of the nursing department.

"If the physician is your customer, then your operational philosophy becomes the physician, like any other customer, is always right. You notice I said 'operate.' I did not say 'believe.' Nobody really believes the customer is always right. How could you? Retail doesn't, service doesn't, and nurses don't. But if you operate this way and understand why you're doing it, you can create a rationale that you can live with. The customer's ego also gets the massage it requires. It enables you to avoid a lot of the internal wear and tear that resentment creates."

"Clients are so frustrating to deal with because they're so critical to your business. Whatever they do or say is given overblown credibility and importance," says Jean Meader, a quality control auditor. "You can't get angry with them and expect them to keep coming back.

"I try to cope by remembering what works with other difficult people—with bosses, co-workers, subordinates, and my in-laws. What works is refusing to take what they say personally.

"If you focus on the project—what needs to get done and what's required to do it—or on the product, or on the service, I believe you're on safe ground. Don't defend yourself—but do stand up for the company or the company's policy. If you don't get personally defensive, and you don't attack the customer on a personal level you've got an even chance for success.

"Male clients expect more attentive service from women," says Ina Jaworski, a travel agency client representative. "They may believe in their hearts that men are more competent, but they do not expect that another man will wait on them. Some, however, expect that a woman will—or at least that she should.

"Even my male colleagues have some pretty weird notions for this late in the twentieth century. One of them recently complained to me that women have an unfair advantage in our industry. When I asked him what that might be, he said, 'you can always use your sexuality to charm customers.' The implication was, I guess, that he had to work for his sales."

Manipulators

"I try to treat all my customers professionally, but when I begin to sense I'm being patronized or manipulated by a male customer it really makes me angry," Ina says.

"There's a type of customer who tries to set himself up as knowing more than you do. One I dealt with, insisted he's been in the travel business himself and he knew he was entitled to better rates than the ones I'd gotten for him.

"I really felt like I was in a bind. I wanted to tell him to get lost in the worst way, but you can't keep your job by turning customers away.

"So I tried to diffuse the situation by asking him questions–innocuous questions about whether or not he could plan his trip during the off-season, whether he could stay longer, or if he'd consider a charter flight. I just kept them coming, and I was as pleasant as I could be.

"I listened politely to each of his reasons for not being able to follow one of my suggestions.

"He had no problem asking me for special consideration. Could I bend or break the rules in some way just for him? It was embarrassing because I knew he would never behave like this in front of another man–he knew he wouldn't get away with it, so he wouldn't even try it.

"Still, I remained firm, but pleasant. I let him know that I truly wanted to help him, that I valued his business, but there was no way the systems could accommodate what he wanted me to do. I never allowed myself to get angry or to cave in any way.

"Holding your ground like that can be a big boost to your self-esteem. At least it was to mine. I kept telling myself that I'm the one in control. I gave him room to back down with some degree of dignity and eventually he did just that.

"We retained his business and I didn't feel at all diminished," Ina says. "Oh, it was difficult to get through alright, but I felt a surge of confidence after it was over. He seemed fine too. I guess he felt it had been worth a try. He'd probably dealt with some pretty compliant women in his travels, at least before he met me!"

Second Opinions

Architect Sonja Lyle says that what upsets her most is when male clients "research my advice." "Recently," she says, "I was working on an expansion project for a new hospital wing. I worked with the building administrator for weeks on the design, the structure, and the cost. We were about ready to close the deal when I found him checking my work with one of my male colleagues.

"I was furious. I couldn't let the client know, but I really let my colleague have it. That wasn't a particularly good solution. It helped for the moment, but now I'm left with a work relationship that needs repair.

"It just gets so frustrating, to have to prove yourself again and again. I'm a good architect. My boss thinks so. My fellow architects think so. My repeat clients think so too. It's not my work that keeps getting questioned. It goes deeper than that. It's my gender–me. Sometimes a new client will look at me and I can see the wheels turning in his head: 'Can a woman possibly do this?' Well, yes, a woman can. And I do.

"I've learned a lot since that incident," Sonja says. "I'd handle the whole situation very differently if it happened today. An attorney friend of mine, Helen Chen, read me the riot act when I told her about it.

"Helen suggested I take the chip off my shoulder, stop watching men's reactions so closely, and open my mouth. 'You're the expert,' Helen told me. 'The same men who make judgments about you still need the expertise you provide. That's why they came to your firm in the first place. You have the support of your long-term clients, your boss, and your colleagues. How much support do you need?'

"If this ever happens to me again," Sonja says, "I would confront the client directly. That would certainly be preferable to taking all my anger out on my colleague.

"I'd calmly tell the client that I understood he went to

another professional in my firm for a second opinion. Then I'd suggest that project be turned over to my colleague.

"I'd act as if I was prepared to make all the arrangement for transferring the account and that I believed a transfer would be beneficial for everyone involved.

"Putting the client in a position where he would have to request that I continue to handle the project while I appeared to be making the transfer simply to accommodate him, would place me in a very strong position. It would allow me to win both respect and public acknowledgment from a once dubious client."

Old Assumptions

Alice Hershey is a newly appointed partner in the same architectural firm. "I'm working with a firm right now," she says, "under a lucrative contract which I negotiated with an old friend who is now CEO. We worked together twenty years ago and remained friends. I know our friendship was a major factor in my getting this contract.

"They assigned a staff engineer from the firm to assist with the project. This guy was in danger of being fired. He was really bad. Why they assigned him to me I'll never know. Maybe they just wanted him out of their hair.

"When I refused to change the specs on a model recently–simply because it could not be done, despite my client's desire for a domed atrium– this little pipsqueak said to me, 'You don't have to do anything you don't want to, do you? It must be a good feeling, being a kept woman.'

"This junior nobody, who was in trouble, who was very close to being fired, had no problem saying something like that to me. I wonder if he would have said it to a man who was a partner in an architectural firm, who had the ear of the CEO, and who was at least fifteen years older than him. I don't even have to wonder . . . .

"At first I reasoned that my problem was not with my client but with a member of his staff. The more I thought about it, however, the more absurd that sounded.

"My problem was indeed with a client who was both an old friend and the decision maker who assigned this engineer to me as his liaison for the project.

"Surely there was a more experienced, not to mention pleasant engineer who could have been assigned to me.

"One of the reasons I was invited to bid for the job was my friendship with Ted. The reason I got the job was my firm's expertise in this type of architectural work. This was not a tradeoff–although it began to smell like one to me.

"One of my oldest conflicts surfaced–'Be grateful for the favor Ted gave you, shut up and cope with the engineer,' the little angel whispered in one ear. 'You're a professional. Ted dumped this loser on you for some reason–find out why and fix it!' The little red devil shouted in my other ear. I listened to him.

"I went to Ted. 'He's a son of one of the board members,' Ted began.

"I wouldn't care if he was your own son," I replied. "Take him off this project. I can't imagine what kind of college gave him an engineering degree and I don't want him around.

"'I thought if anyone could deal with him you could,' Ted offered.

"'I won't do it,'" I cut him off. 'I'm not a wet nurse. You hired me to do a job that I'm very good at doing. If you awarded my firm this contract out of friendship and a hope that I'd mother that monster I'll be glad to release you from our agreement and you can start again.'

"Ted was speechless. 'Alice, I never . . . .'

"Maybe not consciously," I said, "but you would never have assigned him to a man. He'd be eaten alive and you wouldn't have wanted to deal with the aggravation. Ted, he needs firing, but that's your decision. My decision is that I'm not taking him on.

"I didn't lose a customer and I didn't lose a friend either. I set what I still believe were reasonable limits with Ted. I didn't allow anger and resentment to build up. I acknowledged that Ted might not have planned this deliberately or consciously but it was still a problem for me. Finally, I offered him an escape route to save face if he wanted one."

Malcontents

Betty Strauss deals with another type of client. Betty is a psychologist who works as a counselor for an employee assistance program for a large corporation. Her clients are both the corporation and the employees it sends to her for referral and counseling.

Jody Raymond was referred to Betty by his foreman. Jody's job was in jeopardy because of his ongoing inappropriate behavior. Jody came to work late, fought with his co-workers, was sent home twice for coming in drunk, and had the worst attendance record in his unit. Jody had been on probation twice in the last year. Counseling was the last chance for him. He had lasted only because, according to the foreman, he worked like six men when he was "on the beam." The negatives, however, now outweighed the positives.

From the first meeting with Betty, Jody was irritable and surly. He did not want to be a part of the counseling process and made it very clear that he was complying only to keep his job. Jody missed appointments, requested rescheduling at the last minute, and accused Betty of being against him just as every one else in his life had been.

Betty, like Jody's foreman, saw a lot of potential in Jody. She allowed him to vent for several sessions hoping for some opportunity for change. It didn't happen.

Jody became more abusive. He told Betty she could not help him, that no one understood him, and his boss was jealous of him. She listened for a few more weeks. Still no improvement. Jody was not open to suggestion, refused to accept responsibility for his situation, and Betty was beginning to feel like a sponge.

Jody may be my client, she reasoned, but we're just wasting each other's time. Part of wisdom is knowing when to give up . . . .

"I tried a different approach," Betty says. "I agreed with Jody.

I told him he was right. I couldn't help him. Maybe his boss was jealous. Maybe no one was supportive of him. Maybe he needed to resign before the inevitable happened.

"Things," she says, "began to change from that moment on. It seems that Jody didn't want another therapist and he didn't want to leave his job. He began to work on his problems . . . .

"Real craziness," says Betty, "whether it's working with clients, customers, or family is using the same approach with people time and time again, failing time and time again, refusing to change your approach, and expecting a different outcome."

Cultural Obstacles

"Dealing effectively with clients requires more than sensitivity–which women certainly have, and more than a willingness to accommodate–which women have too much of," says David Connors, an investment banker. "It requires a mindset that can transcend all expectations of reasonable human interaction. It requires an attitude of accepting short-term frustrations as a kind of investment in longer term growth.

"For example," Dave says, "there is no doubt that there are certain industries where women are not accepted when dealing with clients. The issue disturbs me, but I don't really know what to do about it. I have discussed it with clients. I have personally lost two clients because I used female teams. Dismissal of women as decision makers in business is part of the dinosaur dynamic in some male egos, but it's also an integral part of some cultures.

"Some of this we can overcome, some I'm not so sure. Banks, for example, have changed. If you walked into a bank fifteen years ago with a team that included women, the senior banker would turn up his nose. Now banks are filled with women in managerial positions."

Cassandra York accepts what Dave says, but she is concerned that women are still being asked to "understand," are still being asked to accept unequal treatment as an "investment" in the future.

"Once," Cassandra says, "I remember a client asked to have me taken off the account because he felt I was too young. I was twenty-eight at the time. I honestly believe if I had been a man either it would not have been an issue, or the bank would have been supportive.

"Oh, they told me they wouldn't allow the client to do this. My boss said he would go to the mat for me on this because I was so valuable. Well, in the end I was taken off the account. After all, they told me, it was the client's money. But I felt betrayed.

"The client had referred to me as 'that young girl' and it stung. Eight years of postgraduate education, and six years experience in investment banking and all he could see was some 'young girl' trying to keep up with the big boys. I think if I had been a twenty-eight-year-old male I would at least have been referred to as a young up-and-coming 'man' who maybe needed a little more experience or polish—certainly not a young 'boy.'

How far do women allow the behavior of clients to erode their self-esteem? Women may already be dealing with a variety of other workplace issues like harassment, promotional obstacles, organizational politics, and outright discrimination. What are the limits? What makes sense when the need to maintain both your self-respect and your paycheck is critical? Ultimately it's an individual struggle and an individual choice.

Judith Akita, an insurance agent, says that when clients make impossible demands or act condescendingly toward her she used to get very angry. "My heart used to beat fast, my hands trembled, and I got very defensive. It always ended badly.

"Today I try to detach. I let my customers rail while I observe them and try to imagine what kind of zoo animal they remind me of. Over the years I've been treated to great apes, boars, hyenas, snakes, and parrots!

"Usually by the time I've decided on the animal, the tirade is over. Not responding to an attack has certainly paid off for me. Once my customer has said his piece I steer the conversation toward what I can actually do for him. Sometimes I've even turned a heated customer around—just by listening and saying nothing! If he knew what I was actually thinking!"

"There is no secret to keeping customers happy," says June, who is an entrepreneur in the escort business. "People have always wanted to feel acknowledged, listened to, and important. It's so seldom that people are treated with kindness in the normal course of business anymore.

"Customer service," she says, "has only become a business buzz word since good manners and graciousness began to disappear from our dealings with each other.

"In the escort business my clients are mostly married men. Why, you might ask, would a married man pay between $200 and $250 an hour for another woman's company? Simple," Jane says, "because he wants to be the center of attention for a little while."

In their 1991 book, *Workplace 2000: The Revolution Reshaping American Business,* Joseph Boyett and Henry Conn observe that customers require much more than a program and a promise. June knew this instinctively. Boyette and Conn state, "Customer service, we came to understand, was intimate—the direct customer/employee relationship. It also involved feelings and perceptions on the part of the customer. Unlike speed and quality, superior customer service was difficult to quantify and often even difficult to describe. In the final analysis, it was the way each employee viewed and related to each customer."

June agrees, but puts it more succinctly. "Basically," she says, "all anyone wants is to be taken care of."

June is right. The role of the customer service professional is to take care of customers. Specifically, to take care of the customer's problem or complaint and to solve it in a reasonable way. Taking care of business and taking care of people sometimes get confused.

Because customer service is a very individual and intimate relationship, as Boyett and Conn observe, it is subject to all the usual interpersonal male and female relational struggles in a highly intensified and immediate way.

Some men expect a very different level of customer service from women. Men who relate to women in a sexual or strictly role-defined way (as mothers, sisters, daughters, and lovers only), expect less professional but more attentive service from women. These men, suffering from any of the several manifestations of what we've labeled "the male ego," expect that when they become the customer of a woman she will appreciate them, take care of them, and make sure they get exactly what they want.

The burden, unfortunately again falls on the woman to sort out these demands and address them in a way that allows her to both maintain her self-esteem and keep her job. She must tactfully change the equation between herself and her male ego-driven customer.

The irate customer is every customer service worker's problem. The male ego is a special challenge for women who hold customer service positions.

The key, as it has been in so may instances of coping with this ego, is competence. Treating all customers with one set of criteria, deflecting inappropriate requests professionally, refusing to be intimidated without becoming defensive–these are difficult but necessary skills to master.

In Conclusion

The dilemma a woman faces in trying to cope with a male ego-driven client is to defend herself against his behavior and protect her self-esteem while maintaining enough goodwill to keep his business. It is a very schizophrenic position.

Succeeding as both a woman and a professional is important to a woman's self-image. Fending off a proposition, handling a put down, addressing patronizing clients while keeping an account and ringing up the business–that's winning!

The women of this chapter shared their experiences with hitters, manipulators, and malcontents, those who questioned their capability and authority and those who wanted special consideration. What worked for them was not taking such behavior personally, but focusing on the project, product or the service they were providing, setting appropriate limits, and in some cases refusing to respond at all. The need to provide the customer or client with an escape route to maintain his self-esteem also was considered essential.

10

Moving Up

*"If the world was a logical place, men would ride side
saddle."*

Rita Mae Brown

"Promotion can be a nightmare," says Jane Neely, who
eighteen months ago, became the first female vice
president of her travel services firm. "It's hard to manage the
first few months after getting a new title.

"I'm the only woman in a group of seven senior managers,"
Jane says. "Management meetings began on a regular basis
six months ago. Initially, I was not included. I had to fight to get
in. 'You already report directly to me,' the president told me.
'The other VPs are all out in the field. I can keep you posted on
what goes on at the meetings.' Do you believe it?

"I opened a New Jersey branch office for the firm. I took the
bus to Jersey every day for a full year. We were successful
from day one. So, I went to the personnel department and I
asked what the criteria was for a company car. I was told there
was none. It was strictly the president's call–the man who'd
promoted me.

"The personnel director proudly told me that he had a car. I just stood there looking stupid. But everything came to me like that. There was always a lot of resentment. I have had to find out what was due me by searching and even then I had to fight for it–whether it was a place at the management meeting, an expense account, or a company car. Everything I pushed for I eventually got, but no one offered it."

Obstacles

"Promotions tend to bring to the surface old fears and old feelings," says Lenora Whitney a manager at an outplacement firm. "Like so many of our responses to workplace issues, our feelings about promotions and about work itself are rooted in the way we were raised to view the world."

The obstacles to female promotion include glass ceilings, our own hesitancy to ask for promotion because of fear of being turned down or losing a good relationship with the boss, and our preference for working hard and waiting for recognition. The barriers to enjoying and maximizing a promotion once it has been earned include anxiety, guilt, and fear of envy and conflict. "Old stuff" as Lenora observed.

Envy is a terrible, destructive emotion. In her recent work, *Jealousy*, Nancy Friday says that "Envy is all about spoiling things. At the bottom, it's a desire to destroy."

Some of us have felt the sting of the envy of others as we made our way up the ladder. Many of us have also experienced it in ourselves as others have gone up before us. It is a paralyzing emotion. It can make us sick.

Some people experience the success of others as a personal attack. Petra Lopez, manager of a furniture outlet, says that she and a male colleague vied for the manager position for almost six months.

"The manager was retiring and Artie and I who both worked in sales began what I thought was a healthy and spirited competition. It was something less than good fun, however when I was appointed to the position.

"I guess he really believed he'd get the job. I know that if he did we probably could have continued a good working relationship, but when I got it he went crazy. Artie didn't speak to me for a week. He simply ignored me, pretended I wasn't even there when I approached him in the cafeteria.

"When I actually moved into the manager's office and met with the sales force, Artie sat slumped in his chair and sullen. When the meeting was over, I heard him saying to one of the other salesmen, in a voice so loud I knew he wanted me to hear, that he wondered if his chances would have been better if he'd been a woman, or if he'd been black.

"Artie made my life pure hell for the next six months. He seemed to expect more proof than my boss did that I could handle the new job. He pushed and pushed for special consideration and confronted me at meetings as often as possible. The first change I made in the firm as manager was to fire him."

Self-Preservation

Amy Kinnear is a senior sales representative who is being considered for a promotion to regional vice president of sales. She was asked to put together a presentation of a new line of shirts for a promotion to an important client. Two days before the presentation is due, Amy has not begun the project.

"I'm frozen," she says to Jaime, the shirt designer. "Every time I sit down to put this together I go blank. I've only got two more days left. If I blow this I blow my chance for division manager."

"Is that what you want?" Jaime asked.

Amy turned on him angrily. "What's the matter with you?" she asked. "Of course it's not what I want. Can't you see I'm a bundle of nerves!"

"Look," Jaime said, "this is easier than a lot of projects you've done. You know this line better than anyone, except me. What would be so terrible if you did a bang-up job?"

Amy paused to think about it. She was still annoyed at Jaime, but he did have a point. This was not a hard job. She also knew there were colleagues of hers who would resent another of Amy's "bang-up" jobs and who would have a hard time with her promotion.

Eddie, another sales rep, five years older than Amy, has worked for the company ten years longer then she has and attended a more prestigious college. Eddie thinks that he should be the divisional vice president. The only thing that separates them is Amy's top-flight sales record.

If I screw this up, Amy reasons, I give Eddie the job. Then I don't have to worry about fighting with him, dealing with his envy, or justifying my promotion. That was it!

Amy flushed and looked at Jaime. "I think I just got inspired," she said.

Sometimes women discount their success or ascribe promotions to good luck or good timing. Like Amy, we may not be aware that what we are really doing is trying to protect ourselves from conflict with male colleagues who are in competition with us for the top spots. Sometimes we'd rather give up than face dealing with the anger of those who have been left behind or those who feel threatened by our success.

"At the risk of sounding like a broken record," Lenora says, "it comes down to a sense of entitlement that we don't have and men do. Promotions are earned and granted as rewards for accomplishment. Men understand this. Men believe they deserve promotions. They expect them. If they don't get them they move on."

Knowing Your Worth

Leonora believes that women persist in seeing promotions as gifts, the kinds of gifts, she says "that should be returned when the relationship goes sour."

"Many women believe," Leonora observes, "that if they are not extraordinarily successful after gaining a promotion they have failed. Some of us still feel like intruders into male conclaves who should be grateful for admission.

"We place enormous pressure on ourselves. We do more than we're asked to do and when we wake up to discover we're being exploited we get resentful."

Jane Neeley, the vice president of the travel agency says, "Young professional women with entrepreneurial skills must begin to realize that they make their own success. They must stop feeling such obligation to their bosses and their companies for the 'opportunities' they were given. Most have paid their companies back tenfold.

"I stayed too long at my company. I bought into the message that I was only as good as I was because they supported me.

"There's no harm in evaluating your work environment like you would any other relationship. We can get lazy in a relationship and just stay to be comfortable. Both a relationship and a job environment can become sick–and you can get sick if you stay in either.

"Discomfort and low self-esteem keep people stuck. You have to know your worth. You can be sure your boss knows it. In a work environment, as in a relationship, you can become a shock absorber. It will waste your time and it can deplete you totally."

Anne Minor, a television producer, says she's always been afraid of change. "Change depresses me," Anne says. "I find any kind of readjustment terrifying. Each time I was promoted I was afraid I would not be able to compete at the higher level. I was afraid they'd tell me I didn't belong and throw me back into the junior ranks. It never happened, but I still worry.

"Charlie Packard, a colleague who was promoted at the same time I was seemed to me much freer in the new job. He seemed to be able to enjoy his success in a way I wasn't able to. He didn't obsess about every move he made, and he seemed very comfortable moving right into the producer's circle. I didn't sleep soundly for a full year afterward."

"Success on the job can move you away from other successes–like a happy family life," says Dawn Thomas, a media buyer. "It's hard for me to admit, but I wonder sometimes about the price I've had to pay for my success. My last promotion cost me a long-term relationship that I would rather have kept.

"Women have been accused of fearing success," Dawn says, "but for many of us it's not success that we fear, but loss.

Promotions bring many good things into our lives, but they also bring loss.

"We can lose a reputation for being 'fun,' or lose an image of ourselves as patient and generous. We can lose relationships–not only personal relationships but relationships with friends, peers, and subordinates. As power changes in a relationship other aspects of that relationship change too.

"As girls," she says, "we were taught to define success in terms of productive and happy relationships. It seems more natural for men to define success in the terms organizations use–'struggle,' 'winning,' 'prize.' We have had to learn that organizational success comes with a price–and that price is often what we consider our most treasured successes–stable and satisfying relationships."

Being promoted can bring up old fears of being abandoned–of being punished for daring to move too far away from the traditional feminine role. This can be unconscious, but still very powerful.

Adjusting

"Adjusting to my last promotion was painful," says Gwen Knowlton, a social worker for a state agency, who was recently promoted from a caseworker to a casework supervisor.

"I had to teach my staff how to deal with me, and that was very difficult. A lot of resentment was generated.

"After the promotion people began to complain about my being unavailable. I had a lot of meetings to attend. But women are expected to be accessible. It's hard for me to believe this would have been an issue if I'd been a man.

"It was doubly difficult because I was assigned to supervise a group of caseworkers who had been my colleagues. They initially had problems with my assigning and evaluating their work. They expected me to respond to their needs in a way our old boss, who was a man, never had.

"The women expected me to understand when there were problems at home and to adjust their workload accordingly.

The men expected I would consult with them before making any major policy decisions.

"The hardest part for me was neither the work nor the new responsibility. It was redefining and rebuilding relationships with my subordinates and my colleagues. That was exhausting."

The Boss

"Promotion can also be difficult when the boss won't let go," says Daphne Hudson, who was recently appointed assistant comptroller of an electronics firm.

"I was promoted to a newly created position, but my boss, the comptroller, continued to deal directly with the people who were supposed to report to me. This relationship was comfortable to them and suited everybody just fine–everybody but me! I found myself increasingly out of the loop.

"When I spoke with him about it he said he thought he was helping me. When I told him it wasn't helpful he got angry. He threw back in my face the fact that I had told him how overworked the department was, and I began to feel stupid. I began to feel like I was the one who had done something wrong.

"When I look back, it makes me so angry. He went around telling the big bosses how he believed in promoting women and yet nothing really changed in the department. He was still calling the shots and I was getting a little extra money for doing my old job.

"It was important for me to move ahead and so I decided to struggle with him over it. Finally he told the accountants to report to me, and he authorized me to hire two more staff accountants to relieve the workload.

"Well, his expectations rose in direct proportion to the additional staff. I was never able to catch up. He wanted more and more reports and more and more extensive analysis done. The daily work kept falling further and further behind.

"Now he tells me I do nothing but complain. He tells me I have to be more productive. He doesn't understand why I can't get things done, especially since he's 'given me everything I've asked for!'"

Daphne was able to forge a solution by engaging her boss in some problem-solving strategies. He began to realize the limits of what her staff could reasonably accomplish.

Each morning she brought a list of the tasks she was responsible for to his office. She asked him to help her prioritize them. She told him that the bottom four tasks would have to be put on hold.

The controller did not like it, but he saw that every task Daphne committed to was accomplished. Each task she placed on hold she completed within a reasonable time.

Eventually they developed a productive working relationship and the controller stopped dealing directly with Daphne's staff. He allowed Daphne to manage on her own terms and the job was done—and done well.

Promotion and Harassment

In February 1992, *Working Woman* magazine distributed a sexual harassment survey to its readership. Among other findings, the results released in the June 1992 issue included the following: It appears that the higher a woman rises in a corporate hierarchy the more likely it is she will be harassed.

Those who reported being harassed at higher levels attributed it to men feeling threatened by their promotions. They believed that men thought harassing behavior would deter these women from moving further up the hierarchy and other women from moving in.

"Women need to understand that when they are promoted over a man they must expect a certain degree of resistance and develop ways to cope with it. It can be done. Men don't take criticism well when it comes from a woman. It is important to anticipate this will happen," says Antonia Pointer, an antiques appraiser.

"Don't criticize unless you are ready for an argument. Many men are not good about accepting advice or constructive criticism from a woman. Their adrenaline starts to pump at the thought of a woman, who was once a colleague and is now in charge, daring to question them. Their competitive instinct takes over.

"I tried to help one of our buyers assess the way he was dealing with the customers," Antonia says. "We had grown up in the business together and I moved on to become an appraiser. We're in a very sensitive business. We deal with a lot of people who are used to being catered to and expertise is not always enough. The buyers are experts, of course, but they also need to show sensitivity and patience.

"This guy took every honest effort I made to talk with him about his approach as a personal challenge. He counterattacked, he made excuses, he put all the blame back on the customer—he did everything but listen. Who was I, after all? My promotion must have resurrected every insecure feeling he'd ever had.

"It wasn't until I put him in charge of 'special purchases,' a made-up title that gave him some distance from the other buyers, that we were able to work together again on something like an even keel. He wasn't a bad guy, and he was a very skilled buyer, but he couldn't get past the new equation my promotion had created.

"The distinction I created for him seemed to help him work through the situation in a way he could accept. I didn't want to lose him, he was very valuable to the firm, and in the end I didn't have to—I just had to give a little."

In Conclusion

Promotion, which should be an occasion to celebrate, is an open invitation for male ego flare-ups. It can bring up envy, conflict, and anxieties about loss of close relationships. Women who are promoted into an all male group or promoted over a male colleague can experience real trials.

As men and women compete for the same positions and women begin to win more of them, some men react with anger and a powerful sense of insecurity.

Women must be cognizant of this reaction and not play into a man's sense of insecurity. If you respond by becoming depressed, resentful, or anxious you waste energy that might otherwise be spent on realizing your dreams. Don't get distracted.

11

The Firing Line

> *"It takes as much courage to have tried and failed as it does to have tried and succeeded."*
>
> *Anne Morrow Lindberg*

When He Fires You

*R*obin Tagliani was a business agent at the national headquarters of a large labor union whose locals represent employees in every major city in the nation. Robin and Jack Frankl, the chief operating officer, worked for Fred Davis, the president, for ten years.

In a year when union memberships (and dues) began to decline, and when locals lost more elections than they won, the Board of Trustees took quick and decisive action. Fred was fired.

Jack was appointed "acting executive" and remained in that position for six months. He and Robin had an excellent working relationship and Robin hoped that Jack would be appointed to the presidency. Jack was efficient, well organized, and responsive. He ran the operation with precision and enthusiasm.

The board, however, wanted a complete change of administration. Jack was not appointed.

Robin told him how disappointed she was and asked what he was going to do. He looked surprised. "I'll stay right here," he said. "I'll go back to my old job." She asked him if that was possible, and he assured her it was. "I've always done a good job in operations and I can be valuable to the new guy. Everything will be fine." Robin wondered.

Mark Landau arrived three weeks later. He was polite enough, but cold. At senior staff meetings he seemed enthusiastic about his plans for the organization. He engaged the other managers in his planning, but never asked much of Robin or Jack.

When Robin spoke to Jack about it he told her it would take time. Mark changed the organization chart so that Robin reported to him. He did this without consulting Jack. Again Jack assured Robin this was not unusual. "Organizations are structured in different ways," he said, "and your position is one that you can make a case for reporting to either the operations officer or directly to the president. Actually," Jack said, "it may be more beneficial for you to report to him."

Robin did not think so. The whole situation felt wrong to her. Mark became picky, critical, and eventually overtly hostile. At staff meetings however, he was careful not to attack her.

Robin tried to talk with Jack about the situation, but he was becoming irritable. She wanted to discuss what she thought was a real blind spot in Jack's evaluation of their predicament.

"Can we talk about this?" she asked. "We've worked together for ten years, can't you give me ten minutes? We need to talk, something is wrong."

"Just do your job," he said. "You can't be fired if you do your job."

Robin gave up on any discussion with Jack, but she put her résumé back into circulation and called a few headhunters. She felt so estranged from Jack and wondered if maybe he was right. Maybe she was making more of a problem. Maybe she did resent not being able to work for Jack anymore and was just being difficult.

Soon, however, Mark began to criticize her writing skills. Robin was responsible for communication with the union's locals. She sent them monthly newsletters and periodic legal briefings. Writing was her strongest skill–it always had been. Mark simply told her that her material lacked imagination. Now Robin was sure she knew what was happening. Still, Jack was skeptical.

Finally, Mark retained a consulting firm for a "management audit." It took only six weeks to complete. Jack, as chief operating officer, was invited to the summary session as was the CFO and the other program managers. Robin was not. Mark fired her the next day.

Robin was livid. Before she left the building she burst into Jack's office. "You son of a bitch," she began, "thanks for the support after all these years." Jack looked at her as if she had lost her mind. "I just got fired as if you didn't know," she said bluntly. He slumped in his chair. "I didn't know . . . ."

"You're the chief operating officer of this organization and he fired me without telling you?" Robin asked in amazement. Jack nodded. "I'm so sorry," he said hoarsely.

"Jack," Robin said, "watch your back."

Robin was working again in a few weeks. Sending out the résumés had paid off. Jack, however, was not so lucky. Despite continuing to do his job–and do it well–he was fired two months after Robin.

Robin and Jack are prime examples of male–female miscommunication in the workplace. Robin's intuition signalled that trouble was approaching. Jack's method of handling his own anxiety was to withdraw and to minimize Robin's concerns.

Robin read Jack's withdrawal as criticism and began to question her own perceptions. Their communication deteriorated so thoroughly that in the end Robin was sure Jack knew about her termination and that he might even have agreed to it.

They could have helped each other through a bad time if each had been able to break out of some very gender-based coping styles. The result was that each went through the loss of a job alone after working ten years together.

When You Don't Know Why

How do you know when it's coming? Women get fired for many reasons, among them personality conflicts, a boss who wants to make his "own hires," and pressure within the organization for change. Gross incompetence and misconduct will certainly get you fired, but it usually takes no skill at all to see that coming.

"I was stunned," says Billie Chapin, a textile sales manager. "I didn't even realize where the conversation with my boss was going until it was over. He called me to his office and said, 'it's time for us to talk about separating.' I had no idea what he was talking about—we weren't having an affair! He kept pacing back and forth behind his desk, very nervous and distracted.

"Finally I asked, 'What are you saying.' It took forever for him to explain that he was saying I was fired."

Sometimes the process of removing a competent, but "in the way," employee is so subtle that the person being moved doesn't get the message. "How could they not know?" Bosses ask in frustration.

Yvette Covey was an investment banker who had survived two corporate mergers in three years. She had reported to five different managers in thirty-six months. It was stressful, but Yvette was grateful to have kept her job as she watched so many of her fellow bankers disappear.

Yvette's new boss, Wayne Sharpe, was a dynamo. He told the staff he wanted to build the best division in the firm—in the industry—and he needed their help. He referred to them as the "survivor squad" and said he was thrilled to be managing "the best of the best" of three firms.

Wayne sometimes seemed impatient with Yvette. He snapped at her during a deal but apologized so profusely later that she dismissed it. He met with her during their first six months together and seemed vaguely dissatisfied with her performance, but Yvette could not get any real clarity from him.

"What is it you would like me to do that I'm not doing?" she asked.

"Look, it's the market too," he said. "I'm frustrated that we weren't able to do better this quarter than we did this time last year."

It seemed reasonable to Yvette, still she was disturbed by receiving what she knew was a smaller increase than Wayne had given her other colleagues.

"What would I have to do for you to rate me 'outstanding'" she asked, "so I'll be eligible for the year-end bonus?"

"Don't worry about a bonus," Wayne said (and the implication for Yvette was that he would take care of it) "just watch the trends closely. And don't worry about performance ratings—you're as good as your last deal. The rating system is overinflated anyway."

Yvette was confused, and she could not get Wayne to focus. She sensed he was uncomfortable as she pressed him. He clearly was not going to give her the information she asked for. She made a mental note to bring it up again. She never got the chance.

"Wayne was being critical, I knew that," she says, "but it was all so general. He qualified everything he said to me. Things were 'partly' my fault, or it was a function of the bad economy, or the firm's policies, or my colleagues . . . it was all so vague. In retrospect, I guess he thought he was softening the blow, but he confused the hell out of me."

The blow came three months later. By this time Wayne was very clear and very irritated that Yvette had not gotten the message.

"I don't know what I could have done differently," she says. "Either the decision wasn't totally his, or he was so conflicted about it that he couldn't be honest with me."

Janice Hollings, Yvette's colleague who also lost her job, disagrees. "Wayne wasn't trying to soften the blow, and he wasn't conflicted," she says. "He just couldn't handle criticizing a woman. Most of the bosses I've had find it difficult.

"They suggest, they start to criticize, then back off. They tell you you'd be happier somewhere else, but they never seem to be able to tackle the problem head on, like they can do with another man.

"I've worked for organizations where bosses will call a job freeze, change titles, transfer, or demote just to remove a woman they are uncomfortable with. Anything but face her honestly and directly.

"Men hate confronting women. Even though women have the reputation for avoiding confrontation, I'm telling you that men hate it more–unless it's with another man. Then it's okay."

We won't always get a clear and consistent message from a boss who wants to let us go. Even asking directly won't always get you an honest response.

A good strategy is to ask for a review in writing. If Wayne's concerns about Yvette's performance were genuine he should have been able to give her written feedback. She might have asked him to set objectives to help her bring her performance into line with his expectations.

If she really was being maneuvered, she could have created a "stall" with this request while she put her résumé on the wire.

If you ask for a review and don't get a response, request it again. Let your boss know–by telling him–that if you have to ask a third time you are prepared to make the request in writing with a copy to both his boss and the personnel department. Even if everybody wants you gone, nobody wants to be responsible for provoking a lawsuit.

When You're Caught in the Middle

Lillian Calloway told us that her first professional job was assistant to the facilities manager of a manufacturing firm.

"Frank Barnes saw a lot of potential in the smart, wide eyed, young woman he'd hired," she said, "and he told me that if I could keep up with him I'd have a great future with the company.

"That's all I needed to hear. Initially my job was to follow Frank around, take notes, and serve as general factotum. That lasted about two months. Frank was willing to give me whatever I was willing to take on–and I wanted it all. I took all kinds of courses to learn all I could about operations management.

"In six months I was managing the administrative staff and by my second anniversary I had purchasing, traffic, and maintenance reporting to me. Purchasing and traffic were a cinch, but Charlie, the chief building engineer, took one look at me and said no.

"Charlie was forty years old and deeply resented reporting to a twenty-eight-year-old wiz kid–especially a female wiz who knew something about HVAC systems. He balked every time I asked to see his reports.

"'Don't take any guff from Charlie,' Frank warned me. 'You've got to toughen up if you want to be a manager. Charlie is an insubordinate son of a bitch and has been since the day he walked in here. Getting rid of him would be a feather in your cap.'"

Lillian laughs, "How anxious I was to please Frank in those days! I was in a big hurry to move up and he was my very first mentor.

"But I was super sensitive to any criticism–implied or otherwise–about not being tough enough. I knew I was capable, but I was afraid I wouldn't be taken seriously. I was five feet tall and soft spoken. Frank assured me that if anything could hold me back it would be my style.

"Frank prided himself on being a tough and decisive manager. 'Everybody knows I'm the boss,' he'd say. 'And that's the image you've got to project if you want to stay in control. Once they think you're soft, it's over.'

"So I tried to show Charlie who was boss, but when he and I locked horns he went over my head to Frank. I always knew when he had because I'd hear shouting coming from Frank's office and Frank would be a bear for the rest of the day. Frank hated confrontations with Charlie.

"After each episode Frank would come to my office and tell me I'd better learn to control that son of a bitch or he'd take the

supervision of maintenance away from me. 'Use your authority!' he'd bellow. 'If he's insubordinate, fire him. I'm tired of
dealing with him every time you tell him something he doesn't
like.'

"When I suggested that Frank refuse to see Charlie it only
made him angrier. 'I won't refuse to see him,' he said. 'I expect
you to fix it so he won't ask to see me.' I thought I understood
my marching orders pretty well. I told Charlie to sign up to
take a mandatory training seminar on some new equipment,
and he refused. I told him I would write him up for insubor-
dination. He laughed and walked off the job that afternoon. I
fired him the next morning.

"Congratulating myself on forging a single solution to my
toughness, Frank's discomfort, and an impossible subordinate, I went upstairs to update my boss.

"Frank was livid. By the time I reached his office, the president, Gideon Pilot, had him on the phone asking for a complete
explanation.

'How could you do such a thing without asking me first?'
Frank wailed. He actually wailed," Lillian says.

"Because you told me . . . ." and then Frank lost it. "I never
told you to fire the bastard," he thundered. "I told you to take
care of the problem.

"I beg your pardon," I said slowly, "but you told me that
getting rid of Charlie would be a feather in my cap. You told me
you would support me, that I needed to get tougher with him,
that . . . but he didn't let me finish. 'You went too
far . . . what was your hurry? . . . Pilot hired Charlie himself. You'll just have to take him back.'

"I couldn't believe what I was hearing. Frank paced back
and forth behind his desk. 'I know I told you to be tough, but for
God's sake where's your political savvy? I can't support you on
this. I have to overturn your decision. If I don't Pilot will, and
I'll look like a jackass. You know I can't look like a jackass.'

"I asked Frank to explain to the president how impossible
Charlie's behavior was and how Frank himself had often
considered letting him go, but Frank refused. I said that Charlie should be accountable for his performance just like every-

one else, and asked how I would ever have any leverage with him if I was forced to take him back?

" 'You'll just have to figure that out for yourself,' Frank told me. 'Let's hear what you come up with tomorrow morning to fix it. I assured Gideon it would all work out.'

"I was in trouble. Sandwiched between male egos and given the task of salvaging a working relationship with a boss who refused to support me and a subordinate who refused to take direction from me. I didn't know what to do. A wise woman would have run for her life . . ." Lillian laughed.

How would a wise woman cope?

The first thing Lillian did was to replay how she arrived at this dilemma in the first place. She attempted to mirror male ego behavior when she began to "get tough" with Charlie. She believed it was what Frank wanted and she believed it was a requirement for success. It didn't work.

Then Lillian tried to confront male ego behavior in Charlie by challenging it head on. She attempted to "win" by eliminating Charlie, her opponent. That didn't work either.

She realized she had ignored the role the boss's boss could play in a job action. Charlie's performance was never the real issue. Charlie was a protected employee, and Lillian had never figured that out.

Frank never meant Lillian any harm, she was in fact his star. Frank's empty threats about Charlie were just attempts to salve his own ego because he knew he would never be able to take any direct action against Charlie. It was now clear to Lillian that Frank never imagined she would take action against Charlie either. He assumed she was "not tough enough."

If Lillian was to come out of this situation whole she had to successfully cope with two irate male egos and preserve her own ego in the process.

Lillian forged a face-saving solution from her own concern that Charlie's performance needed to improve and that his attitude needed to change. She knew he must have additional training in order to get certified to operate the new equipment the plant manager had ordered. Charlie had always been recalcitrant about accepting retraining. To continue to manage his area, however, he would have to be retrained.

When Lillian met Frank the next morning he was very uncomfortable. "You're right about Charlie," he mumbled, "but we can't fire him. What have you worked out?"

Lillian explained about the retraining option and recommended that if Charlie agreed to cooperate he could return to work. She asked Frank to support her in making clear to Charlie that if he did not get certified there would be no choice but to let him go. It was a basic requirement of his job. She agreed to take him back on probation.

Frank picked up the phone and called Gideon. "Charlie's staying," he said quickly, "and Lillian is on board." He explained that Charlie had to train on the new equipment to keep his job and that he'd come back on probation. The boss agreed. When he hung up the phone Frank turned to Lillian and looking relieved said, "You'll handle this with Charlie . . ."

Lillian stayed at the job for another year. She was learning too much to leave too soon. She took a very valuable lesson with her to her next job. "Sometimes the male ego is less than meets the eyes," she says.

When You Have to Move On

Robert Lee, co-chairman of the outplacement firm Lee Hecht Harrison, observes in the organization's newsletter "Compass," that "job loss tends to bring out the best and the worst in people."

He cites four common, initial reactions people have to being fired. Some, he says, get depressed. These are the people who blame themselves for being fired. Others deny their situation. They hope for, and perhaps even believe, that "something will turn up" without any effort on their part. They try to minimize what has happened to them.

Still, others panic. They become hysterical and focus on the possibility of never working again.

Finally, some fixate on taking revenge on the person who fired them.

"All four responses are natural," Lee says, "but it is important for an individual to recognize how he or she is reacting and not let it last too long or get in the way of a productive job search."

"In fourteen years of running an employment agency I have yet to meet the woman who was fired who did not blame herself," says Jewel Burnette. "My first words to every female client are, 'get over it.' Men blame everyone else. They curse their bosses, their colleagues, and their customers and they move on. Women tend to wallow in their misery."

Curt Kendall, a career counselor agrees. "Women unconsciously make the workplace a second home," he says. "They form strong relationships with their colleagues and subordinates, invest too much of themselves in their positions, and when they get fired it's more than the job they lose. Some women are convinced that they've let themselves and everyone else down when they get fired. It's terrible to watch."

If you fall into this trap, the result of your termination will be the loss of something you would be much better off keeping–not your job, but your self-esteem.

The fact that women tend to blame themselves for being fired is directly related to our tendency to distrust our own perceptions when they differ with those in authority over us (usually men).

Look at Robin, she knew she and Jack were on their way out. Yet she wondered if his perception that she was "making more of the problem and being difficult" was more accurate than her own.

Women are afraid to be labeled hysterical. We are afraid to be accused of "overreacting" in any situation.

"What will stop a woman?" asks Anne Wilson Schaef in her book, *Women's Reality.* "Tell her she is sick, bad, crazy, stupid, ugly, or incompetent. Most women have been trained not to trust their perceptions and they rarely have the opportunity to explore them without being criticized or dismissed."

Anne Schaef's point is that women continue to back off from the way they see the world. We are too ready to make allowances, too quick to plead "guilty." This not only handicaps our ability to cope with a difficult situation, like being fired, but it may in fact contribute to it. We may create a self-fulfilling prophecy in some instances by our passive behavior.

For example, when a crisis emerges men usually respond by looking for the cause (*i.e.*, the "someone" who is to blame). "Didn't you check?" he asks. "Who was the last one who logged in before the shut down?"

Women, on the other hand, tend to look inside. "What could I have done differently to avoid this?" she asks. "Did I say something that I shouldn't have?, Did I delegate to the wrong person?"

When the situation is highly charged and one person (male) is looking for someone to blame while another (female) is ready and willing to plead guilty, what do you think is going to happen?

It is important to admit that you are wrong or responsible when you are. But, if this is your starting point on nearly every issue you will undermine your own credibility–and that is self-defeating.

It is also self-destructive to wallow in guilt, blame, and/or depression when you do get fired. The truth is, many times the person who has been fired never knows why. Unless you know for a fact that you were grossly negligent or incompetent–and even then it's more productive to figure out how to correct this for the future–it is time to move on. Grandpa was right: get right back on the horse once you've been thrown. If you think too much about it you might convince yourself that you never really liked riding anyway.

When You Fire Him

What happens when a work relationship breaks down and you are compelled to discipline or fire a male subordinate?

Kay, in Chapter 1, learned that firing a male subordinate can require all your time and energy–especially when he appeals your decision on the basis of a special relationship he's forged with your boss.

Jeanette, also in Chapter 1, learned that not taking the time and energy to address and solve a problem with a male subordinate can leave you in a far worse position.

"Dave always resisted taking direction from me," Jeanette says, "even when he was new on the job and my confidence in him was very strong.

"When I'd ask him to contact specific donors or request input from certain staff members he would always alter the list just a bit. He'd drop a person, add one, or try to negotiate another time frame. At first I thought he was just being overly conscientious, but when his responses became predictable I realized what he was up to.

"Dave was readjusting our status. Oh, technically I was his boss, but he edited every directive of mine so he could maintain a sense of autonomy and not feel diminished by having a woman telling him what to do.

"I ignored too much of his outrageous behavior. I hoped that eventually he'd cooperate if I treated him with what I called 'respect.' It wasn't respect at all, it was avoidance.

"Talk about denial! I suggested, coaxed, joked, and took him into my confidence on issues. I did everything but clearly tell him that if he continued to run all over agency policy I'd fire him.

"All my interactions with Dave followed the same dance routine. He'd re-confirm his status as the direct mail expert; I'd agree; I'd give him direction; he'd modify it. He'd lay out a series of problems he was having with his female colleague, ask me to intervene, and then make requests for special consideration for himself–time off, major expenditures, etc.

"Instead of supervising him I negotiated with him and my compliance with his requests must have seemed like submissiveness. Our relationship became unbalanced.

"I treated him more like a colleague than a subordinate and it should have been no surprise to me when he preferred that arrangement and responded as a colleague. I must have appeared incompetent and insecure to him–less for what I said then for what I left unsaid.

"If I had used the same behavioral criteria for him that I used for my female directors I would have fired him. I should have been willing, as Kay was, to address the problem directly and firmly.

"When his staff came to me with complaints about his behavior I should have reviewed each incident with him and demanded an explanation. That's exactly what I would have done with the women.

"I catered to his ego, which was silly, inappropriate, and ultimately tragic. His ego was his problem. My responsibility was to manage my division and solve problems no matter who caused them.

"When he missed staff meetings, cancelled appointments, and left messages saying he was spending a 'day in the field' I should have addressed each incident immediately and documented conversations about my expectations of him.

"Each time I ignored a deviation from acceptable behavior it became worse the next time. First he took donors to lunch and charged the agency, then suppliers, then colleagues, and finally subordinates. He acted as if he worked for a conglomerate instead of a small agency.

"I should have told him that although his skills were very valuable to the organization, clearly his behavior had to change.

"When he began to run over budget I should have shut him down. I had the authority to approve or deny all budget over runs in my division.

"Finally, if he continued to freelance his operation I should have put him on final warning. If he continued beyond that, I should have fired him.

"I spent more energy mollifying him and justifying myself to the other directors, that in the end no one had respect for me and I had little left for myself."

Firing a male subordinate may be uncomfortable, but if you focus on applying the same criteria for all your subordinates, if you ignore assaults on your capabilities and fight old tendencies to defer to male anger it can be done effectively and professionally.

"I have fired women who have cried and cried in my office," says Deborah Lyons, a banking executive, "and I've come through fine, but let a man begin to attack my credibility and I feel diminished and, yes, even guilty. Still, I get it done.

"When a relationship with a male subordinate breaks down and separation from the organization is required, some men will question your ability, your motives, your ethics and your judgment. Some will resent your authority, deny any responsibility for the events that led up to your decision, and will seek revenge by going to your boss–especially if your boss is a male."

Kate Albright, controller for a marine research foundation, said that an accountant she fired went to her boss, the chief financial officer, and tried to convince him that Kate was guilty of bending accounting regulations for favored colleagues and stealing from the firm.

"It was humiliating for me to even dignify those charges with a response," says Kate, "but clearly revenge was his intent."

Remember George in Chapter 7 who was fired by his boss Lydia, but refused to accept it and went on with business as usual? George could not believe the company could have invested such authority in Lydia and he decided he'd wait her out until someone with *real* authority recognized his value and reinstated him!

Frances Segal, publisher of a trade journal, had a similar problem with Ted Fields, a technical editor on her staff. Ted had been in his position for twelve years when Frances was appointed. He was one of four senior editors who reported to her.

From the beginning Ted appeared to be enthusiastic and cooperative. He was outgoing and popular with the staff. Frances was relieved by Ted's willingness to accept change in the division. Some of the other editors were upset and resistive of the new administration.

Soon, however, it became evident to Frances that what Ted made up for in enthusiasm, he lacked in depth. She would assign Ted work, he would eagerly accept the task and that would be the last she heard about it until she asked him for a status report.

There was always a reason Ted couldn't get the work done. He had an emergency, another deadline caught up with him, he delegated some of the task and his staff was not able to complete it, and on and on and on. Ted also had the annoying expectation that Frances would understand.

Ted was full of excuses, but he had no real sense of accountability for the work Frances assigned him. She began to feel like they were playing some sort of crazy game. "I'm being 'yessed' to death," she thought, "and there's never any outcome."

Ted considered himself a key member of the editorial staff and considered it his responsibility to instruct Frances in the history and culture of the firm. When they met to discuss his progress he always attempted to get the subject off himself and onto the fascinating history of the firm. Frances wondered how any manuscript had ever gotten published in the past. She knew Ted had to go.

"Firing Ted was a wrenching experience," Frances says. "He was a very likable guy. If he was my neighbor, cousin, or colleague, I would have enjoyed his company very much. But I could never get a day's work out of him. Being his boss was maddening.

"In the end Ted appealed to every emotion he thought he could arouse in me. He said he was sure he could never find another job, that I was harder on him than I was on the female staff, that I was jealous of his long history at the firm and was afraid he wanted my job. When nothing else worked he cried.

"He told me he thought I had more compassion than to fire him after his long service and his willingness to help me. He really thought I could be manipulated or shamed into changing the outcome. Ted never once accepted responsibility for not producing one solid piece of work in the eight months I tried to work with him.

"He left my office a very angry and bitter man. I'm sure I was the subject of many tales he told to his friends about how impossible it is to satisfy a female boss."

When you are compelled to fire a male subordinate, it's helpful to remember that status is a larger component of most men's identities than it is most women's. While we all know that when we accept a job our fate in that workplace is put into the hands of our boss, when the boss is female it makes some male subordinates feel very insecure, at times diminished and often very angry.

In Conclusion

Being on either the delivery or the receiving end of the firing line is never easy or pleasant.

Being fired is often difficult to anticipate and sometimes one never reaches a clear understanding of why it happened.

When a female supervisor is in a position where it becomes necessary to fire a male subordinate she should focus on the situation, the performance, and the behavior, and not allow herself to be deflected by any of the various manifestations of the male ego. In an attempt to alter the outcome some men will question a female supervisor's ability, her motives, her ethics, authority, and judgment.

The most common emotional response to being fired is for men to blame outside factors for loss of their job, while women tend to look inside and feel responsible.

Whatever your response has been to firing someone else or to getting fired yourself, the most important lesson to be learned from the experience, is to refuse to be stuck in self-absorption as well as self-pity, and to *move on.*

12

Last Words

"There are no shortcuts to any place worth going."
Beverly Sills

Gender Challenges

*R*epeatedly, we have heard threads of the five gender challenges woven into the tapestry of a woman's experience in the workplace. How many of these ring true for you? Can you add others?

CHALLENGE #1–The workplace is still a man's world. This is not because men are better, smarter, stronger, or more entitled, but simply because they are the ones who created it, and they still hold the positions at the top.

CHALLENGE #2–The male ego is less formidable than we think, and the female ego is more resourceful than we anticipated. Women tend to underestimate their ability to deal directly with the male ego.

CHALLENGE #3–Women and men are different. These differences will continue to fuel interpersonal difficulties in the workplace. Each believes that if the other would only change his or her behavior the workplace would be less stressful.

CHALLENGE #4—The workplace will never be sexually neutral. Sex will always be a factor in the highly charged and competitive atmosphere of business.

CHALLENGE #5—Women's collaborative, cooperative managerial style has begun to ease out the male model of power and control. Female styles are rewarded as males adopt them; then men move up the corporate ladder faster than women.

These gender challenges will confront, confound, and coalesce women throughout their careers. However, the task at hand is to understand their subtext to shape workable strategies to override them. This requires paying attention, listening carefully to the spoken and unspoken, reading body language, and grasping the politics of your situation. It helps to analyze the dynamics of your interpersonal interactions with men—those who are difficult and those who are not. Taking time out to take stock of what is going on can help you blunt or divert some gender-based capriciousness. It can also help you figure out what is working for you and what is not. Knowing your part in an interaction can lead to changing course and using your understanding of the relational domain/dimension to your advantage.

There are many facets to a circumstance and various options along the path. What impact will each decision have if you aim to move toward mutual gain, or if you aim to win, or if you aim to retreat. The point is you decide the route rather than having it determined by another.

Jeanette, Kay, Gail, Cindy, Moira, and Rose have shared their attempts to cope with the male ego. Let us look closely at how Moira used her own resourcefulness to turn less than a positive encounter into a learning experience.

MOIRA

Moira began her new job of project manager at a retail firm with enthusiasm. Her previous boss had given her a great recommendation and her new boss, the vice president, was particularly pleased to have such a smart woman on his team.

Initially, the vice president assumed responsibility for Moira's orientation. He liked her quickness, her ability to design systems, and her seemingly good rapport with her workgroup.

This was the first time she had supervised a group of people and she felt a little self-conscious. They would test her individually and as a group. She learned that she had to be overly observant of her staff's individual behavior. She kept journals on her individual relationships. Through trial and error she developed a repertoire of different approaches to each person. She also asked the vice president for advice, and he was flattered to be put in the role of expert.

During staff meetings the vice president began to banter with Moira, smile at her comments, and make her the center of his attentions.

Moira loved the job and its challenges. The vice president gave her several plum assignments. She worked long hours to complete them ahead of schedule. He took her on three business trips within her first three months.

She liked the vice president. He had offered good advice on how to handle a difficult staff member and he had helped her work through a complex marketing strategy late one evening. She saw him as a good resource and as a credible mentor. He had shared with her some of his frustration on the job and had invoked her sympathy. Then he began to make passes at Moira which she tried to ignore or overlook.

She found herself defending him at meetings. Once she encouraged the group to hire a facilitator to handle their planning session so it would be easier for the vice president to think along with them rather than be burdened with facilitating their process and thinking simultaneously.

The vice president allowed her unlimited access to his office and engaged her in more intense discussions of plans for his workgroup and confidences about the staff. Gradually, they were on the precipice of an affair.

A colleague invited Moira to lunch. She told her there were

rumors throughout the company that she and the vice president were having an affair. She explained how distressing that was to their workgroup and its effect on the group's morale. The vice president had a penchant for office affairs and his behavior was watched closely for any inkling of a dalliance. He had a reputation for making promotions difficult for women.

Moira was stunned, but tried to cover her upset. She thanked her colleague for her candor. She assured her that she would try to figure out a way to salvage the situation.

Her conversation with her colleague was like a wake-up call. The depression and dismay she felt after having left her previous job when the affair with that boss ended and having been rejected by her colleagues were experiences she did not want to repeat. This was a job she wanted to keep and where she wanted to succeed.

She tried to figure out how to overcome the situation and handle it so the vice president would not be so upset that he would retaliate if she did not succumb to his advances. She hoped to accomplish this so that he hardly noticed.

Moira called her best friend and together they worked out a strategy which aimed to preserve a decent working relationship with the boss and serve Moira's ambition to succeed. Her friend insisted they write down everything that Moira knew about her boss's personality so they could play to his ego needs and avoid behavior that would aggravate her situation.

Her boss had scheduled three late afternoon meetings with her to discuss the progress of her project. She asked his secretary if she could have one long meeting instead of three short ones. She asked that the meeting be scheduled first thing in the morning.

When the vice president asked her about the meeting change, she explained that she and her group had developed a presentation that needed more time and his input. She wanted to be sure they had plenty of time so they could incorporate his ideas. The vice president accepted her explanation and enjoyed the flattery.

Moira and two members of her staff made a spirited presentation to the vice president. She was careful to keep everyone focused on the work, as well as to make sure that the vice president's ideas were central to the discussion. Moira knew this was a man who needed lots of approval, recognition, and smiles.

After the meeting, the vice president asked if Moira would remain a moment. He told her that hers was a great marketing strategy and that he was very proud of her. He invited her out after work to celebrate.

She thanked him and said she would love to, but she had promised to help her group put the finishing touches on the video which would accompany the presentation. She invited him to join them for a toast about 7 P.M.

The vice president felt a bit stymied, but said he would stop by if he were in the building. He did not show up.

The vice president had scheduled a three-day trip for them that would extend into the weekend. She knew she had to come up with a very cogent excuse to avoid traveling alone with him. She began to talk with him about including others of her staff in the out of town meeting citing their need for development and exposure. He resisted at first, but left the decision up to her. She arranged for her project assistant to accompany them.

Moira wanted to offset the rumor that she was having an affair with her boss. She debated whether to discuss the rumors with him, but decided against it fearing he might misread her upset as an invitation to pursue the affair.

She did not want him to feel so angry with her that he would push her out of her job or pass over her when it came time for a promotion or a bonus.

Very gradually, Moira shifted her attention away from the vice president. She spent more time with her workgroup and invested time in developing relationships with her peers. She made sure her group produced outstanding work that made the vice president look good and advanced his agenda in the company.

She played to his need for flattery and attention by keeping him informed, playing up his ideas, and laughing at his stories. She tried to keep their meetings task centered and pretended that she did not recognize his attempts to personalize their relationship.

A few weeks later she placed a photograph of herself with a very attractive man on her desk. The vice president wandered into her office, picked up the photograph and said "congratulations." Moira smiled, handed him a polished document and did not miss a beat. His behavior become less familiar and more professional.

Relearning

Men are being pressured. Their power is being eroded and they don't like it. Who would? Resentment is something women in the workplace of the 1990s and beyond will have to manage.

Challenging your competence, excluding you from the decision making, staring at your breasts, restating your comments as their own are the interpersonal attacks you fend off as you cope with the male ego in the workplace. These are behaviors designed to keep those in power in power and those storming the gates, at bay.

You understand that. You want to level the playing field. You do that by always being prepared, knowing who you are, and understanding the individual profiles of the men who influence your work life.

Nobody concedes easily. The workplace will require changes of women and men. Relearning ways of relating to each other will be our mutual challenge in the workplace. Socializing our young for gender parity will be our responsibility.

Women are talking with each other about the best ways to cope with manifestations of the male ego. They are learning to be strategic around these behaviors: to be patient, clever and observant. Women are changing the texture of the interpersonal dynamics. Astute men are paying attention and modifying their behavior. Active relearning is taking form.

Listen to yourself, no matter how frightened it makes you. All the information you need is inside you.

How do you listen? Ask yourself what your changing, growing, expanding, curious, sensitive self is craving right at this moment? Now ask what your fearful, dependent, guilt-ridden, anxiety-filled self is holding on to right at this moment? Begin to examine what is most important to you, what you really want, and accept that to get there you must make choices.

Your competence and ability to conquer yourself embolden you to transcend the male ego. It's your race. Clear the hurdles!

A lifetime of jobs-well-done is the ultimate reward.

Index

ing self-esteem, 30; and women's success, 57, 69
Competition in men, 36, 46
Compromise as female strength, 76
Confidentiality, standards of, 32
Conflict: with colleagues, 129–33; and Ninjutsu tradition, 130–33; and promotions, 150, 152
Conflict resolution, 81–83; and colleagues, 129–33; in management, 27
Confrontation: and firings, 164; and the male ego, 30
Confusion of men and sexual harassment, 64–65
Conn, Henry, *Workplace 2000: The Revolution Reshaping American Business*, 146
Consensus in team building, 41, 83, 119
Control: by bosses, 94–96; and Japanese managers, 78–79; need for in men, 78, 88; and power, 8
Coolidge, Gail, 115
Cowboy mentality, 22, 77–78, 80
Cultural norms as obstacles to women, 144. *See also Female socialization; Male socialization*
Customer service, 137, 146–47
Customers. *See Clients*

D
Daughters, 18–21
Decision making: as a male strength, 56; and intuition, 72; and politics, 53
Demographics: and women in managerial positions, 102; and the workplace, 25–26, 41
Depression and firings, 168, 170
Discrimination: age and class and race, 23; and glass ceiling, 55; in the workplace, 26, 41
Distractors as colleagues, 128–29
Diversity of workforce, 25, 27, 44, 102
Dumb blonde stereotypes and harassment, 14, 60

E
Earhart, Amelia, 5
Ego. *See Female ego; Male ego*
Elias, Marilyn, 105
Empathy as a female strength, 40, 72
Empowerment: by good bosses, 99; and the female ego, 40; through management, 115
Entitlement: and promotions, 152; sense of in men, 39–40; sense of in younger workers, 25
Environment: evaluating work environment, 153; hostile environment and sexual harassment, 60; political environment and organizational politics, 49–55
Envy and promotions, 150
Equal Employment Opportunity Commission (EEOC), 67
Equal Pay, 43, 44, 69
Equivocators as colleagues, 125–28
Exclusion: from decision making, 181; and the glass ceiling, 55; from power, 40; and sexism, 68, 69

F
Family: companies as extended family, 72; family responsibility differences, 55, 77; and promotions, 153
Fathers as mentors/role models, 18–20
Fear: of abandonment, 154; of change, 153; and harassment, 65; of success, 153
Feedback on performance, 164
Female ego: advantages of, 70–84; and maternalism, 22; resourcefulness of, 29; unique strengths of, 26
Female socialization: and Eastern values, 80, 83; and gender parity, 181; and Japanese management styles, 77–84; negative aspects of, 70; as an obstacle to corporate success, 38–40; positive aspects of, 71, 74, 83, 114–15; and team building, 80–83; and transformational management, 71

Sources

Abouzeid, Pamela. "The New Action-Oriented Therapy." *New Woman*, November 1991, pp. 36–40.

"Are Women Fed Up?" *Time*, October 12, 1987, pp. 68–73.

Arnott, Nancy. "Should You Manage Like A Man?" *Executive Female*, March/April 1988, pp. 20–24.

Astin, Helen, and Carole Leland. *Women of Influence, Women of Vision: A Cross-Generational Study of Leaders and Social Change.* San Francisco: Jossey-Bass Publishers, 1991.

Berkowitz, Bob. *What Men Won't Tell You But Women Need to Know.* New York: Avon, 1990.

Bly, Robert. *Iron John: A Book about Men.* New York: Addison-Wesley, 1990.

Boyette, Joseph H., and Henry P. Conn. *Workplace 2000: The Revolution Reshaping American Business.* New York: Dutton, 1991.

Bramson, Robert M. *Coping with Difficult People–In Business and in Life.* New York: Ballantine Books, 1981.

Carr-Ruffino, Norma. *The Promotable Woman.* Belmont, Cal.: Wadsworth Publishing Company, 1985.

Cohen, Herb. *You Can Negotiate Anything.* New York: Bantam, 1980.

Deep, Sam, and Lyle Sussman. *What to Say to Get What You Want.* New York: Addison-Wesley, 1992.

Domingues, Cari M. "A Crack in the Glass Ceiling," *HR Magazine*, December 1990, pp. 65–66.

Elgin, Suzette Haden. *The Gentle Art of Verbal Self-Defense.* New York: Prentice-Hall, 1989.

Friday, Nancy. *Jealousy.* New York: Bantam Books, 1985.

Gallese, Liz Roman. *Women Like Us.* New York: William Morrow & Co. Inc., 1985.

Gillian, Carol. "In a Different Voice." *Psychological Theory and Women's Development.* Cambridge, Mass.: Harvard University Press, 1982.

Hardy, Marshall, and John Hough. *Against The Wall: Men's Reality in a Co-Dependent Culture.* New York: Ballantine, 1991.

Harragan, Betty Lehan. *Games Mother Never Taught You.* New York: Warner, 1977.

Hays, Stephen K. *Ninja Realms of Power: Spiritual Roots and Traditions of the Shadow Warrior.* New York: Contemporary Books, 1986.

Hite, Shere. *Women and Love, A Cultural Revolution in Progress.* New York: Alfred Knopf, 1987.

Jeffords, Susan. *The Remasculinization of America: Gender and the Vietnam War.* Bloomington, Ind.: Indiana University Press, 1989.

Johnson, Robert A. *He: Understand Masculine Psychology.* New York: Harper & Row, 1989.

Johnson, Robert A. *She: Understanding Feminine Psychology.* New York: Harper & Row, 1989.

Jordan, J., A. Kaplan, J.B. Miller, I. Stiver, and J. Surrey. *Women's Growth in Connection.* New York: Guilford, 1991.

Keen, Sam. *Fire in the Belly: On Being a Man.* New York: Bantam, 1991.

Kolb, Deborah M., and Gloria G. Coolidge. "Her Place at the Table: A Consideration of Gender Issues in Negotiation." *Negotiation Theory and Practice,* edited by J. William Breslin and Jeffrey S. Rubin. Cambridge, Mass.: Pon Books, 1991.

Lerner, Harriet Goldhor. *The Dance of Anger: A Woman's Guide to Changing the Pattern of Intimate Relationships.* New York: Harper & Row, 1985.

Mattis, Mary C. "Dismantling the Glass Ceiling, Pane by Pane." *The Human Resources Professional.* Fall 1990, pp. 5–8.

Margolies, Eva. *The Best of Friends, The Worst of Enemies: Women's*

Hidden Power Over Women. New York: Simon & Schuster, 1985.

Martinez, Michelle Neely. "The High Potential Woman." *HR Magazine,* June 1991, pp. 46–51.

Miller, Jean Baker. *Toward a New Psychology of Women.* Boston: Beacon Press, 1976.

Miller, Dr. Patricia Murdock. *Powerful Leadership Skills for Women.* Shawnee Mission, Kan.: National Press Publications, 1988.

Milwid, Beth. *Working with Men.* Hillsboro, Ore.: Beyond Words Publishing Inc., 1990.

Newhouse, Nancy R. (ed.). *Hers: Through Women's Eyes.* New York: Villard Books, 1985, pp. 233–253.

Newsweek, (ed.) "Drums, Sweat & Tears: What Do Men Really Want?" *Newsweek,* June 24, 1991, pp. 46–53.

Pascale, Richard and Anthony Athos. *The Art of Japanese Management.* New York: Simon & Schuster, 1981.

Peters, Thomas J., and Robert Waterman, Jr. *In Search of Excellence: Lessons from America's Best-Run Companies.* New York: Warner Books, 1983.

Phelps, Stanlee, and Nancy Austin. *The Assertive Woman: A New Look.* San Luis Obispo, Cal.: Impact Publishers, 1990.

Powell, Gary N. "Upgrading Management Opportunities for Women." *HR Magazine,* November 1990, pp. 67–70.

Ralston, Jeannine. "Know Your Enemies." *Glamour,* August 1991, pp. 214–215, 236–238.

Rizzo and Mendez. *The Integration of Women in Management: A Guide for Human Resources and Management Development Specialists.* Greenwood, 1990.

Rogers, Louisa. "A Woman's Place." *Entreprenurial Woman.* December 1990, pp. 46–49.

Schaef, Anne Wilson. *Women's Reality: An Emerging Female System in a White Male Society.* San Francisco: Harper Books, 1981.

Shamer, Laurence. "Do Men Like Independent Women?" *Glamour.* August 1991, pp. 209, 234–238.

Steinem, Gloria. *Revolution from Within: A Book of Self-Esteem.* New York: Little, Brown, 1992.

Tannen, Deborah. *That's Not What I Meant.* New York: Ballantine Books, 1986.

Tannen, Deborah. *You Just Don't Understand.* New York: Ballantine Books, 1990.

Tannenbaum, Joseph. *Male and Female Realities: Understanding the Opposite Sex.* San Marcos, Cal.: Robert Erdman Publishing, 1990.

Tausky, Curt. *Work Organizations.* Itasca, Ill.: F.E. Peacock Publishers Inc., 1978.

Tec, Dr. Leon. *The Fear of Success.* New York: American Library/Reader's Digest Press, 1976.

Thornberg, Linda. "Working Toward Change." *HR Magazine,* June 1991, pp. 52–55.

Walker, Paul L. "The Glass Ceiling." *Employee Assistance,* Vol. 1.4 (August 1991).

Weinstein, Bob. "The Enemy Within." *Entrepreneurial Woman.* October 1990, pp. 50–53.

Williams, Bryn (ed.). *Martial Arts of The Orient.* London: Hamlyn Publishing Group, 1975.

Wolf, Naomi. *The Beauty Myth.* New York: William Morrow, 1991.

Wolfer, Karen S., and Richard G. Wong. *The Outplacement Solution.* New York: John Wiley and Sons, 1988.

"Women: The Road Ahead." *Time,* Special Issue, Fall, 1990.